JOURNEY ROUND JERSEY

Front cover photograph (Robin Briault): the author,
Mike Stentiford and Bodie at La Pulente

Lighthouse at Corbière

JOURNEY ROUND JERSEY

*Coast and conversations: ninety
encounters on a fifty-mile walk*

Robin Pittman

(author of *Speaking of Jersey*)

Illustrations by Jefferson Randles

Maps by John Syvret

SEAFLOWER BOOKS

Published in 2005 by
SEAFLOWER BOOKS
16A St John's Road
St Helier
Jersey
JE2 3LD

Origination by Seaflower Books

Printed by Cromwell Press
Trowbridge
Wiltshire

Typeset in 10/13 point Plantin

ISBN 1 903341 28 0

Contents

Introduction

Jersey's coastline measures almost 50 miles and is walked each year by 1000 or more Islanders taking part in the charity event organised by Itex (Jersey) Ltd. I have once done the circuit, which entails climbing and descending several thousand feet, in a reasonably respectable time of 17 hours. My tour of the Island for this book was somewhat more leisurely – a year and a quarter.

The result is a not too detailed guide to Jersey's shores and, perhaps more significantly and relevantly, an account of my encounters and conversations with 90 of those who either live on the coast or have an interest in it or a business there. They have a story to tell about its varied character and features and their involvement with it. Many have also been willing to give me their reflections on the Island today and what living in Jersey means to them.

There are precedents for books that describe circular journeys. Tim Robinson's *Stones of Aran: Pilgrimage* published in the 1970s is an atmospheric depiction of the coast of the largest of the three Aran Islands that lie off County Galway. More recently Iain Sinclair's *London Orbital* describes his long walk skirting the 120 miles of the M25 motorway. My reading of these two books inspired me to embark on my own circular journey. There is also a precedent for waylaying large numbers of willing people, conversing with the Dictaphone running and subsequently writing up the result; this has been the life-long method of Studs Terkel, nonagenarian Chicago journalist, resulting in a whole series of absorbing paperbacks exploring the lives, fortunes and hopes of a wide cross-section of American society.

I have acknowledgements to make. I must first thank two local authors who allowed me to plunder the odd fact or figure from their helpful books. These are Mary Phillips's *Tracks and Tales: 21 Coastal Walks* and Sonia Hillsdon's *The Visitors' Guide to Jersey*. Readers will be able to learn more about these two accomplished writers, since each agreed to talk with me, and our conversations feature in these pages. I have also of course to thank all the 90 who agreed readily (I only had two refusals) to speak to me, none of whom felt too intimidated by the daunting presence of microphone and recording machine. Jefferson Randles has my warm thanks for the line drawings as does John Syvret for the chapter maps, the inclusion of which resulted from the helpful suggestion of Michael Good. I am very grateful to my wife whose advice, encouragement and acute proof-reading have been of the greatest benefit. My final thanks must go to Roger Jones of Seaflower Books whose valued support and remarkable publishing skills have once again lightened my authorial load.

RNP
St Mary, Jersey
August 2005

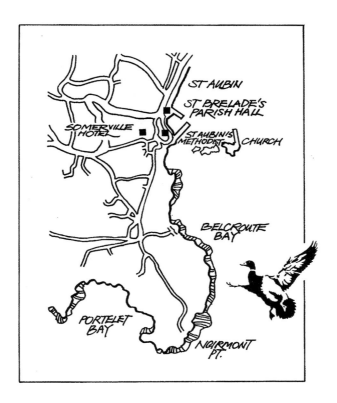

1

St Aubin to Noirmont

It may seem strange to some that a journey round Jersey should start at a railway station or, more precisely, a railway hotel. But here at the St Brelade Parish Hall facing the harbour at St Aubin is where the railway line from St Helier arrived in 1870 before being extended to Corbière in 1884.

From the late 17th century St Aubin was the Island's commercial centre, and the fine merchants' houses along The Bulwarks and in the High Street are testimony to a prosperity based upon ship-building and the trade with the Newfoundland cod banks. Here the fleets bound for North America wintered, with a new jetty built in 1670 and with further harbour developments through the 1700s.

St Brelade Parish Hall

Are we in a town or a village? A moot point. It certainly called itself a town when it had a market building; and one of its colonnades survives in part of the NatWest bank, the rest of it being demolished when the railway was extended from here to La Moye.

I found Max de la Haye, the Connétable of St Brelade, in what was formerly the Terminus Hotel. He thinks that his office was once the bar. The hotel stayed in business for four years after fire destroyed the train shed behind it in 1936 and was then occupied by the Germans in 1940. The parish purchased the hotel for £2000 in 1946 and it opened for its civic purposes two years later.

Mr de la Haye was born and brought up in the parish. His family has farmed there since 1600 and he was a grower until his retirement in 1995. He became active in parish affairs in the early '60s, began as a roads inspector and moved through many civic and honorary police appointments, becoming the Father of the Parish in 1999.

> We're a parish that has changed dramatically since the Occupation. It was quite an agricultural parish in those days, with tourism of course. It is now a very commercial parish, heavily built up. And St Aubin is a very old village – the first harbour to

be built in Jersey – with boat-building and sailing to Newfoundland and the Gaspé for the cod and the mahogany. That's why there's so much mahogany in the Island, brought over from the New World. In area we are the second largest parish and we have the longest coastline – from Beaumont to the El Tico café on the Five Mile Road.

Parishes to me are a very democratic way of running affairs. As Constables we have no power. It is the ratepayers at parish assemblies that take the decisions. We go along with a recommendation and it is the majority decision of the parishioners which stands. I see the parish as an important facet of modern Jersey. It is a tradition that must be preserved. And the honorary police as well; a very useful service – people coming forward, giving up their free time in helping others, and putting something back into society as well.

~

Coming out of the Parish Hall I turned left to Battrick's Boatyard, the domain of Wally Battrick since 1968. I met him only weeks from his retirement, with his premises about to be demolished and a restaurant planned for the site. Until joining his father and brother in the business he had had a career as an electrician, gaining an aircraft engineer's licence and working in the Sudan before coming back to Jersey and specialising in avionics at a time, he says, when aircraft really had to be maintained rather than just swopping black boxes. Made redundant, he joined the family firm when the potential in the Island for the marine leisure industry was considerable. He is someone who has had his own particular vision for the development of St Aubin. His first big ideas were formulated in the 1970s for an 1800-berth marina between the village and the fort which lies offshore.

I put the plans for that in in 1973 and rehashed them again in '82 and '92 when they finally decided to build the Elizabeth Marina which I was not in favour of: on dry land, the wrong place, facing the wrong way, and it's at the bottom end of a commercial seaway. I had my marina plan looked over professionally by an international economist. He crunched all the numbers. Top men looked at the scheme and thought it a brilliant idea. They thought that this here was the place for it, with a ready-built marina village which has everything: 1800 berths in the safest area of Jersey sheltered from the westerly and south-westerly winds. You could get in and out of my marina, not only at half-tide. We could have got mega-yachts here, the big boys with the money. And that's what this island needs. But the scheme got nowhere and the powers that be then used my number-crunching to justify their own Elizabeth Marina which is in the wrong place.

I then quizzed him on his current reclamation scheme for St Aubin, and he told me about global warming, the level of the roadway outside the Catholic church being about two feet higher than in the village itself and the increased flooding dangers from a south-westerly gale. Wally's scheme would be to reclaim land to the east of the harbour wall and, with it, manage the vehicle. He's even invented a suitably impressive set of initials – VMS (for vehicle management scheme) – to give some gravitas to his ideas.

It would move the vehicle off the village – pedestrianise it a lot more and make it far more pleasant. It's in the new Island Plan. I have got some private interests in it which scares me a bit, because I don't want to let go of it. If it gets into the hands of civil servants, and the States being the States, the minute they see a flat piece of land they want to build something on it, and this is not for building on. And there is a jewel in the crown – a 10-metre slipway and we can have dinghy sailing out here again; there's nowhere other than St Catherine's at present.

The States should have done something like this with the B and Q site north of St Helier: a big car park there and a shuttle service of minibuses feeding the Town from the north. There would have been another ideal opportunity in the reclamation west of Albert, with a one-storey car park all the way under that area. You could have cut out a lot of the traffic from the Town. But the States do not have vision, long-term vision. It's a three-year term of office for most of them. The first year they find out how the system works because nobody has done sufficient homework; the second year they try and make a noise; and the third year someone has stamped on them damned hard and put them out. And the civil servants have got everybody stitched up.

~

I wished Wally Battrick well in his retirement and with his plans and took my first tentative steps along The Bulwarks. Within a hundred yards I had come on the Methodist church. Methodism in the Island goes back to 1786, and St Aubin's was the scene of fierce early opposition in Jersey to the Methodist cause. Despite this the movement grew and 1817 saw the building here of a church seating 230. This was superseded by the present building, started in 1867 and at a cost of £2000. Its latest renovations date from 1995 when visual barriers were removed and glazed doors installed, making possible a view of the church interior to the passer-by. In membership it is the largest of the 16 churches that form the Jersey Methodist circuit, and worthy of mention is the fact that, since the opening of the Communicare Centre at Les Quennevais in 1975, there has been a partnership with the two Anglican congregations in the parish.

St Aubin Methodist Church

St Aubin's Methodist minister, the Reverend Ian White, was within months of retirement when I went to see him in his Quennevais bungalow. He was born in Manchester, brought up in Cheshire and had 20 years in Bristol before coming to the Island as Superintendent of the Jersey circuit and District Chairman of the Channel Islands. In addition to all these responsibilities he had just completed a year as President of the Conference, Methodism's nearest equivalent to being the Archbishop of Canterbury.

I was brought up in a rural context. The Methodist church was at one end of the village and the parish church at the other. In the '40s and '50s we had little to do with each other – except on the occasion when we opened our new Methodist church and the Rector came, and this was thought a great honour. Now it would be normal.

As to our ministry at St Aubin, one of our prime purposes is with the tourists. We have 17,000 visitors to the church every year and from May to September they make up a large congregation which goes down to 70 or so in the winter.

Methodism has its special place in the history of Jersey. John Wesley came to the Island in the 1780s, and part of Methodism came here from France. And then the British military bases in Jersey until the early part of the last century also swelled the Methodist ranks. There has been a long tradition of Methodism here; indeed at one time it was the strongest denomination. It was particularly vibrant in the rural parishes and there still remains an element of that today. But now we are going through a period of considerable change and it will not always be possible to minister to 16 churches across an island of 45 square miles.

Another change on its way is the freshly agreed Anglican-Methodist covenant which has a great deal to offer especially in the rural areas. There are several difficulties which will challenge us, not least the fact that the Church of England is so closely interwoven with the Island's civic arrangements. All of us contribute in the rates to the upkeep of the parish church, and some Methodists will feel threatened by the Covenant and the fear that, if there are changes in the use of buildings, then it will be the parish churches that will survive and the Methodist churches that disappear. This gives us a certain anxiety, but we do have Communicare here at Quennevais which has been a successful joint operation with the Anglicans over many years.

As to the future I would describe myself as an optimist with realism attached. I think that God has not finished with the church as an organisation and that there is a new church waiting to be born. At the heart of most people is a yearning to understand life and its meaning, and the church has its contribution to make. I am an optimist provided that the church is willing to let go of the things that hold it back. Sometimes it can be our approach to worship; sometimes we spend too much on buildings. Perhaps we have got the Gospel a little bit upside down from time to time.

Now retirement beckons and I shall be leaving Jersey, an island endowed with so many skills and gifts. Difficult times lie ahead for it; the employment situation, the future of the finance industry creep up on us. That's why it is important for the church to be seen as part of the wider Island community. I shall leave Jersey, having a very positive feeling about it. Just a few niggles of course – but that's life.

~

I resumed my journey along The Bulwarks, coming at the end to the Old Court House Inn with its façade, not so many years past, familiar to millions of television viewers as Bergerac's favourite watering-hole. Here 17th century privateers brought their booty for auction, with an Admiralty judge deciding whether the boat itself and its cargo were or were not legitimate prizes. The spoil from captured vessels required storing and sorting and this house and its cellars was the likely venue for these operations.

With the Royal Channel Islands Yacht Club on one's left, it is a brisk climb up the Mont du Boulevard towards the Somerville Hotel. A previous building was burnt down in the 1880s and a Swiss architect was employed for its replacement, giving it something of the appearance of a Swiss chalet, or so it is said. Or is the effect more Gallic than Swiss? Here is an extract from the hotel brochure in the early 1900s when the train provided a regular link with St Helier:

> St Aubin is fortunate in possessing the twin benefits of a rural, green, leafy countryside at its rear and a commanding clean sweep of magnificent bay with corresponding beaches to the front. The Somerville, with its high situation, stands like a French chateau amid this beauty.

~

The way to Belcroute Bay from here lies either along the beach or inland towards the Route de Noirmont, with a private road above the sea sadly denying one passage. But a drop down to Belcroute is recommended, to the bay where ships from plague ports had to anchor up during their time of quarantine. It is a quiet spot, good for a swim at high tide round a moored boat, with a gin and tonic and a packet of crisps against the sea wall as a post-dip reward. And above is the handsome Noirmont House, built in 1810 and rebuilt 20 years later and where Lillie Langtry spent her honeymoon and reputedly scratched her name, with a diamond naturally, on a window pane. This also is Bergerac country, with the house frontage more than once standing in as Charlie Hungerford's plush abode.

I retraced my steps up to the main Noirmont road and took the half-mile path through the woods at the top to reach Noirmont Point, this impressive headland at the western end of St Aubin's Bay. Noirmont Common is Jersey's war memorial, purchased by the States for this purpose in 1946. A granite slab carries this inscription:

> **THIS HEADLAND WAS ACQUIRED BY THE STATES OF JERSEY ON BEHALF OF THE PUBLIC IN COMMEMORATION OF THOSE MEN AND WOMEN OF JERSEY WHO PERISHED IN THE SECOND WORLD WAR 1939-1945**

Noirmont Point

All around me was evidence of German fortifications. Here was the Batterie Lothringen, built by the Organization Todt and some local labour to keep the surrounding seas free from Allied shipping and attack. Apparently the guns only spoke in anger on a few occasions, one of which was on 13 June 1944 when HMS Ashanti and a Free Polish destroyer were driven off by accurate and sustained firepower.

The Channel Islands Occupation Society has been active over the years in restoring the German gun emplacements, and the authority on all this and leading light of the Society for many years is retired postman Michael Ginns whom I went to see in his St Ouen farmhouse. Mr Ginns had his own experience of the Germans when at the age of 14 and with his family he was deported from Jersey and interned in Bavaria for nearly three years. He told me of the Society's membership of 270 and described to me how it was not so much his time in the German camp but what he saw in Jersey before he was deported that fuelled his Occupation interests. As a boy he witnessed the German re-laying of the railway from St Helier to St Aubin and Corbière and was all agog when they laid a narrow-gauge track at Grouville Common. He is extremely knowledgeable about all the German defences constructed around the coast.

It was a good thing when Noirmont was bought by the States after the war; it saved the area from development. The bunkers there were sealed up in 1948 and this saved them from the scrap merchants. The main command bunker is in good condition.

For the first thirty years after the Occupation nobody wanted to know about the bunkers. But from 1976 when we started as a Society the attitude changed and it was realised that in the long history of the Island they are as important as the castles and the Martello towers. With the guns which we have put back it is the same thing: they are historical artefacts. So long as it is not overdone it is all right.

We have been accused by some of indulging in glorification of these relics; Michael Day, of the Jersey Heritage Trust, wanted us to put up notices saying, 'Men died building these bunkers'. The truth is that a lot of work was done by local labour, and the Island authorities were shouted at and bullied by the Germans in an effort to recruit a larger workforce. A thousand men were wanted for sea wall construction at St Ouen's Bay, and there was a big meeting between the Bailiff and the Germans. It was pointed out that under the Hague Convention no civilian could be forced to do work against the interests of his own side. When the men learned this, fifty per cent of them walked off. The remainder didn't. Patriotism can fly out of the window when money is concerned.

As to our objectives now, we have done what we wanted to do – to restore and preserve the best examples of every type of bunker. But we're getting older and there is great difficulty in finding young people to replace us. Perhaps it may come to our putting the bunkers on a care and maintenance basis and us becoming a sub-section of the Société Jersiaise. We are reaching a crunch point.

~

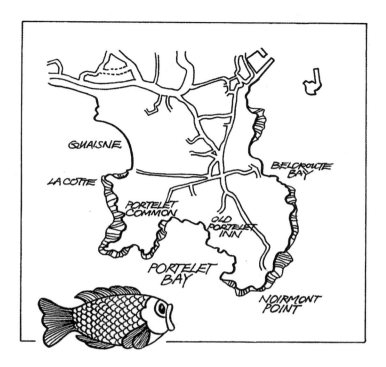

2

Noirmont to Ouaisné

I left the headland at Noirmont with a quick glance skywards. There is an old Jersey proverb: 'Quant Niermont met son bounet ch'est seign de plie', which means, 'When Noirmont wears her bonnet it's a sign of rain'. In fact it was actually a raw afternoon and drizzle was in the air as I set out across the heathland paths to Portelet.

It is not far to the Portelet Inn. Joan Stevens in her *Old Jersey Houses* indicates that it possesses one of the earliest dated arches – 1606, describes the workmanship of the whole façade as of high quality and points out that it is one of the very few old Jersey houses that can be seen from the sea, with most being inland as protection from raids and weather.

On a winter's day Portelet is not too cheerful a spot, with its fields of laid-up hire cars, the site of the hastily demolished Janvrin's Farm and its boarded-up holiday village awaiting redevelopment. But it is a fine bay and there in the middle of it is the Ile au Guerdain, known to all as Janvrin's Tomb. Some say that this is the resting place of Captain Philippe Janvrin who in 1721 died within sight of his home aboard his ship *The Esher*, quarantined off Noirmont Point because it carried the plague. Ian Parker who owns the handsome Portelet House overlooking the bay recounts a slightly different tale.

Above: Portelet Inn; below: Janvrin's Tomb

The story told by my aunts and uncles who were alive when we bought this house in 1971 was that Janvrin was too ill to be brought off the ship and when he died his corpse was put on the island and subsequently moved from there and buried in St Brelade's churchyard. He is said to have owned a dwelling here and we think that it may have been the cottage that now forms part of this house.

In fact the tower on the island is one of those built around 1800 when the coast was being fortified in case of invasion by the French.

Portelet House, with its lawns sweeping down to the beach on the western side of the bay, had been in my sights as I left Noirmont Point. Ian Parker, who bought the Hotel de France in St Helier in 1968 and whose sons Robert and Andrew are now in charge there, has family roots in both Jersey and Guernsey on his mother's side. He told me that he bought his home from the Dewars, the whisky family. It had been unoccupied for some years at a time in the 1960s when gardeners and staff were hard to come by. The cottage at its heart apparently dates from the 17th century, and a major redevelopment of the property took place in 1920. He is not only an expert on the history of Portelet Bay but is someone who has played a prominent part in Jersey's tourism industry.

The Hotel de France was originally built as a hotel but it went bankrupt and became a school run by a Catholic order. It became a hotel again after the war and we acquired it 20 or so years later. And it doesn't matter what business you are in, whether it is tourism or whatever, but you need the commitment and determination to make it succeed.

I am concerned about Jersey's government. You have people in politics here, each representing on average 1500 voters and with no qualifications at all. Some are failed business people who have got into the States and don't understand money. Some have no proper training and don't know the basics. Tourism in the Island has a great future: there's a lot to see and do, good walking, a beautiful countryside. But it would be nice to have the interest from those in the Tourism department and from those who are meant to be doing the marketing.

Now whether there will be a finance industry in the future is another matter, because that is something in an office with a computer and can be easily transferred anywhere. It's a pity too to see agriculture going down. If fields are allowed to rot away or farm buildings deteriorate, then it harms the infrastructure of the Island.

I am not very struck with our present politicians. It all comes down to leadership. Go back to what Jersey was like at the end of the war: the government was then run by people who understood money and it was better run at that. But as to the future I am an optimist. Jersey is surrounded by water; there is pleasant countryside, lots of recreational facilities, swimming, sailing, and so on. It will always be a place where a lot of people will wish to come.

~

I left the bay and strode on to Portelet Common or, more correctly, La Commune de Haut, a wild area of land in the closest touch with the sea. Most of it was donated to the National Trust for Jersey by Mrs Hope Dixon in memory of her father, Jurat Guy Fortescue Burrell de Gruchy, the Seigneur of Noirmont. On its western edge we are high above Ouaisné and also above La Cotte de St Brelade, famous for its paleolithic and neolithic remains. Here excavations have in the past uncovered evidence of at least 20 mammoths, five woolly rhinos and diverse animal and human bones and artefacts. And here the Prince of Wales, while a Cambridge undergraduate, came to a dig as part of his academic course.

Above the cave are the remains of the 18th century Portelet battery, and this magazine, along with some additions, was the home for 38 years until the year 2000 of Mrs Joyce Smith. I thought it would be worth my while to seek her out at her Quennevais flat, and indeed it was.

I am not a Jerseywoman myself but my mother was Jersey. I came here in 1962 for a year and am still here. I came to live in this amazing house. I had met a man at the end of a dog lead and we got talking. And it went on from there, and he said, about our getting married, 'I won't get married until I get that house on the cliff top.' And he went to see Mrs Hope Dixon, and it was all fixed. That was in 1963.

We had no plumbing or electricity. We had oil lamps and oil stoves and no lighting in the kitchen. The water had to be boiled on the top of the cooker and there was no water laid on. When years later there was a drought, the Men of the Trees came with their lorry and its big plastic tank and filled our own tanks for us. We had no toilet; we had to have a caravan toilet.

I lost my husband in 1979 and I stayed on for another 21 years. I said to people, 'I'll be here till I'm 80,' and I just made it. Later I was fixed up with a windmill generator and got a little TV and a strip light over my chair and a spotlight in the kitchen. The shopping eventually became a problem – walking to Portelet corner and then coming back with the carrier bags, sometimes in pretty bad weather.

People remember the goats. I got the nanny in 1976 and the billy two years later. He was like a dog; such a pet. They are so intelligent, goats. They used to wander down onto the beach below and surprise the holidaymakers.

I loved living there – the peace and quiet, the country, and the birds and all the wildlife. Mrs Hope Dixon once said to me, 'I can't think how you can stay there. You're so brave; up there all alone in that place.' I replied, 'I don't think anything about it.' People used to ask whether I got bored with nothing to do. But there was a lot more I could have done if there had been more hours in the day: searching for wood, sawing it up, going down on the beach, taking the goats for a walk over to the other headland.

And a final thought: as long as I lived there, the nearer I was to Heaven. I missed it this past year when I was laid up. I would have got better more quickly if I'd been on my headland. I just loved it so much.

~

From La Cotte Point one takes the steep path down through the quarry to Ouaisné and its common, La Commune de Bas. Down at the bottom, next to the boarded-up restaurant (a sign of the times as far as tourism is concerned) and at the edge of the slipway is Mon Ami, the home of Roy Pinel.

This family home dates back to 1600 and I am over 80 and have lived here all my life except during the German Occupation when they moved us all out. I went to school from here with my sister. As seven-year olds we walked to St Aubin – a good distance there and back again at the end of the school day. The decline in tourism here has a lot to do with people liking a drink when they go out. The Smugglers' Inn is popular, but others wanted more highbrow stuff and it didn't really work. People eat in pubs these days.

My mother ran a little café here – The Rest Tearoom. It was just a small hut really, And most of the people who had bungalows here were business people from Town. In those days there were 30 or so bungalows on the hillside here. They were local holiday homes; people did not go off to Spain or Majorca; they came instead to Ouaisné. It was very popular here before the war – when there was not much else to do. There were two tennis courts, always busy, which had to be booked in advance. And the Rest Tearoom became The Jolly Teapot, and just across from it was another café, The Merry Kettle.

Roy Pinel is an authority on the quarry that lies above his cottage.

In the '20s the quarry was a hive of activity. The trumpet would go to signal the blasting, and we would all have to go inside since there were always a few stones that would shoot from the quarry and land on the roof. Then the stone was hoisted on to the top common by crane and was then loaded onto a horse-drawn cart. Later the quarry managed to get a lease from my mother and they ran a road straight into the quarry itself, and after that lorries used that road. In 1935 a stone-crusher was installed at a lower level, just off the beach, and the lorries would back up and load the chippings there. Of course the dust was terrible, covering all the bungalows and trees. Everything was covered in granite dust. There were public meetings, and the upshot of it was the closure of the quarry. That was just before the Occupation.

The holiday bungalows were all demolished by the Organization Todt; the slave labour would escape and take refuge in them. The Organization Todt never had enough men to control this, and so they knocked them all down. And that was the end of the bungalows. They never were allowed to go up after the war. Some said that it had been a shanty town, but quite honestly I could not see that it was. They had been very popular. The bungalows had been kept well – with gardens in front – and the owners looked after them.

This is the Commune de Bas down here. I am one of the remaining *tenants*; the right goes with the property rather than with the person. The rights date from 1574 but there is no demand for them any more. No cattle are grazed here now; there always used to be cows and goats. And there was a lot more grass in my early days; not as much gorse as there is today and mostly covered then with heather.

~

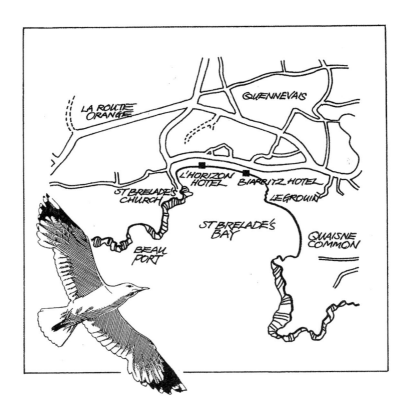

3

Ouaisné to Beau Port

I left Ouaisné and struck out along the German-built anti-tank sea wall that skirts the Common, all grass and gorse and the natural habitat for the Dartford Warbler and Jersey's only species of frog, the agile frog. Of course all this is St Brelade's Bay, and Le Grouin, with its 12th century French meaning of 'promontory', is the pile of rocks that divides its two parts. Behind the promontory is Le Côtil du Grouin, 15 vergees in all acquired by the States in 1856 as a firing range for troops.

One either scales the heights of Le Grouin at high tide or else walks across the sand to come on this lively holiday bay with its hotels and houses and what remains of its fortifications from both two centuries and just over half a century ago. Here is the sandiest of beaches, palm trees, manicured lawns and flower-beds and the Sir Winston Churchill Gardens, with those memorable words from his broadcast of 8 May 1945 – 'and our dear Channel Islands are also to be freed today' – chiselled on a rough-hewn granite block.

High above the bay is the Biarritz, just a little different from its neighbours in being a Methodist hotel and here, sitting in his out-of-season reception area, I found Duncan O'Neill, its lively and positive general manager. He first came to Jersey in 1981, worked in and fell in love with St Brelade's Bay early on, had increasingly senior posts at the Pomme d'Or, the Royal in Town and the Portelet Hotel and was appointed to his present position in 1997, having in the meantime married a receptionist working at L'Horizon along the road. He told me something of the Biarritz's history.

> It was founded 45 years ago as a Methodist hotel by Samuel Ferguson, a wealthy industrialist from the north of England. Ferguson decided that for the causes of Methodism it should be unlicensed, though it is not part of any Methodist chain – not related to any other hotel in any way. We have a board of directors – Reg Jeune is our chairman – and 150 shareholders worldwide.
>
> No; I am not a Methodist myself; very much an Anglican background. But I was appointed to control the business element of the enterprise rather than its particular Christian aspect. Perhaps in the last few years we have made the hotel a little broader in its views, but we consider that it remains distinctive. We open our doors to all Christians – and, in a Christian way, to anybody. At the end of the day it would hardly be a Christian thing to do to give our guests a religious test as they came over the threshold. We've had Jewish people, Hindus and so on, and it would be wrong to shut our doors to others. The Christian element is so-to-speak an extra: we have a daily morning ministry and on Sundays, after a grand buffet, a Songs of Praise. And we run a coach on Sunday mornings down to the St Aubin Methodist church. And of course attendance at these things is absolutely optional; there aren't any head counts!

I then asked Duncan, with his perspective of well over 20 years here in the industry, for his thoughts on the current state of Jersey's tourism. This is what he had to say:

There seemed to be more disposable income when I was young in the early '80s. I remember the time when I was acting as Head Hall Porter at the Pomme d'Or and we had three or four bars and a live band and 400 people, and we would have to lock the doors at 8.30 p.m. in order to stop anyone else coming into the building. The days of packed hotels have gone. And there has been a decline in evening entertainment. In those days there were the Inn on the Park, the Chateau, the New Mediterranean, Caesar's Palace – cabarets going on all the time. Now the alternatives are the cinemas or the pub down the road. Mind you, our customers here – sober persons wanting to avoid organised entertainments - are looking for something a bit quieter.

The big plus for Jersey in my view, its distinctive nature, is safety. With two boys, one aged 6 and the other 3, safety in today's world is a great bonus. We may be catching up with the UK a bit – drugs, Saturday night in Town, a growing fear of violence – but I still feel that Jersey is a safe place, and my beloved St Brelade's Bay is the safest of the safe. That's why I am happy here.

~

I left Duncan and moved along the bay to L'Horizon and was delighted, settled in the lounge and with cups of coffee for both of us 'on the house', to have the opportunity of talking to Justyna Urbanska, one of the many from Poland now working in the Island's hotels and restaurants. Like many of her Polish colleagues she is highly educated, having after school studied sociology at university.

I left university two years ago when I first came to Jersey. I had never been to the British Isles before and I was offered a job at L'Horizon. My reason for coming was to improve my English. I was here for six months and worked as a chambermaid. When I returned a year later they promoted me and made me a floor supervisor.

I knew nothing about Jersey at first but found out as much as I could from the internet. I enjoy the hotel work and I get round the Island during my time off. I like walking and sometimes use a bike or the bus. Corbière and Plémont are favourites for me, and I have a Polish friend at Rozel working in a hotel there and we meet up. I am not sure how long I shall be staying in Jersey but I love the housekeeping. We're a great team and I love the contact with the guests. Jersey is good news for me, and I am hoping that my mother and father will be coming over for a holiday this summer.

~

The parish church, at the western extremity of the bay, was my obvious next port of call. This must surely rank as one of the Island's most impressive and atmospheric ecclesiastical buildings. Built of La Moye granite and dating from the 11th century, it has the sea lapping the churchyard from which to the shore runs the *perquage*, the sanctuary path for those wishing to escape the rigours of the medieval penal system for the alternative of perpetual banishment. And in the churchyard also is the Fishermen's Chapel, 12th century in origin and possessing the Island's finest wall paintings dating from the 14th and 15th centuries. There was an obvious candidate to inform me further about all this, and I made for the Rectory and the Reverend Mark Bond.

St Brelade Parish Church

The Rector first told me of his origins – Torquay and born into a family of wine and spirit merchants. His career was initially in catering, and he thus understands the hotel business. He is himself a church organist, and it was at the end of a Saturday playing for weddings and a Sunday playing for umpteen other services that his vicar asked him why he did not consider doing *his* job. In due course Salisbury Theological College and ordination followed. He came to Jersey in 2002, having been Vicar of Highbridge in Somerset and he is developing various ways in which the Church can work with the hospitality industry for the mutual benefit of both. He terms it 'spiritual tourism'.

> When I was a curate in Taunton we came as a family to Jersey for our post-Easter break. We visited St Brelade's Bay and, standing in the church, I turned to my wife and said, 'I wonder what you've got to do to get a job like this.' And she said, 'In your dreams.' Then years later came this letter from the Dean asking me whether I would be interested, and here I am.
>
> The main body of the church has been standing for a thousand years, and the spirituality, the continuity of the place, is potent. It has a deep spiritual heart; going down into the nave is like entering the Church of the Nativity in Bethlehem. It touches many people, not only the locals, and we counted 20,000 visitors through our doors last year. We are a tourist church and we double our congregations in the summer. Anglicans, Roman Catholics, French, Germans, all come and we try to provide a good standard of Anglican eucharistic worship, and our policy is definitely 'open altar'.
>
> A special challenge to being a priest in Jersey is that of being a 'foreigner': all of us parish clergy are English now. And so you have to approach Jersey with the right sort of open mind and not make UK assumptions. There is here a sense of heritage which England has lost. Take funerals: in England one has to do funerals with few people there because nobody knows anyone. It is more common here to have a funeral with a minimum of 100 present. That indicates 'community', a sense which England has lost. And as Rector I have a part to play in the civic life of the parish, and that is a great privilege.
>
> Religious practice is changing and we have to face up to it, and we have to search for different ways forward and not remain totally locked into Sunday worship. Take Communicare at Les Quennevais, with 1000 people a week using that building. So we

must not get obsessed with questions of church attendance. Weddings, funerals, baptisms are other important ways in which we touch people's lives.

There is a joy for me and my family in our being here in such a lovely place. Every morning, religiously almost, we open the curtains and look out to this marvellous view. But we must guard against being blasé: the Church of England has got to face change and the Island must face change as well; nothing is static any more. The traditional model of the Church has to adapt; we must find different ways of speaking to people in a changing world.

~

My intention after leaving Mark Bond was to wander along the Chemin des Creux, in other words keeping along the western side of the bay and past Le Coleron Battery (which the National Trust for Jersey owns) to the handsome house at the end of the road, Beau Port Battery, the home of one of Jersey's most famous residents, the former racing driver Nigel Mansell. Sadly I had had no reply to my letter asking for a few minutes of his time and I did not have the temerity to ring the bell on the outside of his rather formidable gates. Instead I diverted off the road two hundred yards after the church and up a steep path to inspect the impressive grave of Lord Trent, a.k.a. Jesse Boot, the founder of the chemist chain. Here he lies with other members of his family, the single word TRENT prominent on the edifice and with the inscription 'to love and to cherish' around the base.

I then found the path to Beau Port, toiled up the slope to a magnificent view back over St Brelade's Bay and reached the car park 200 feet above what must surely be one of Jersey's most beautiful beaches. A notice at the car park entrance announced that we were in Les Creux Millennium Country Park, an unhappy recent creation, with paths, unnecessarily 'improved', leading to the wild and fine Beau Port headland. And what on earth is the utility and why the expense of the dressed granite signs in this special area which should have been saved from such intrusions?

~

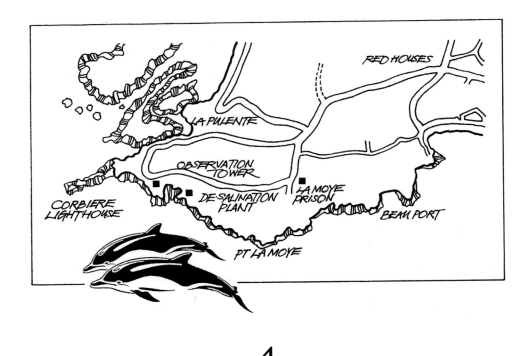

4

Beau Port to Corbière

I struck out west from the Beau Port headland in the direction of the Island's prison and found myself at once on a switchback of coastal paths. The authority on these, and indeed the man most responsible for this fine network on both the south-west and north coasts, is Mike Freeman, who now has the title of the States' Principal Ecologist. I went across to Howard Davis Farm at Trinity where he has his office to see him. Quiet-spoken, tall, pony-tailed and earringed, he told me how he had first come to Jersey in 1972, working for eight years at La Moye Golf Club. After that he was a self-employed gardener until taken on by the States on a temporary basis, building paths and cleaning up the area at Le Mielle de Morville, along the Five Mile Road and north of Kempt Tower. He then studied for an Open University degree and has worked for the States ever since.

My responsibilities now are mainly about recording the wildlife of the Island, giving advice how not to damage it and working out a biodiversity strategy. But I still retain my interest in the footpaths. In the early '80s there was a fair amount of unemployment and the resultant job schemes were very useful for the work we were doing at the time on the north coast paths, creating them and linking up the existing ones, and we had the labour to carry out the task.

The last section before I moved into the office in 1995 was the south-west paths from Corbière to St Brelade's Bay. Conflict with owners is always a particular headache and some people object to the paths: 'I've paid a lot of money for this view and I don't want to share it with anyone.' The problem west of Beau Port was particularly intractable, and I am not terribly happy with the diversions from the old path which we had to create.

Also it is a good thing if we can direct walkers with a degree of subtlety; you don't want an enormous number of signposts; try to keep a sense of exploration and let people discover for themselves. I'm now no longer involved in the countryside management so much, but increasingly I feel that it is better if possible to leave things alone and resist the tendency to 'municipalize' the countryside. It's a matter of taste really.

What am I most proud of over the years? Without doubt the coast footpaths. I am very proud of this achievement, making accessible places that people can really enjoy. And this lovely south-west coast – wild and beautiful – was the last area to be tackled in this way.

~

It was less than a mile along the path, but with some particularly steep steps, until Jersey's prison, La Moye, was reached. Built in the mid '70s and with its massive perimeter fence-cum-metal wall (over which no prisoner has ever escaped), it is a formidable place which has, unlike penal establishments on the mainland, to cater for all categories: those sentenced and on remand, men and women, young offenders and prisoners who are considered vulnerable.

I went to the top and had no difficulty arranging to see the Governor, Mike Kirby, who was regrettably due to return to a prison post in England after a positive three years in charge at La Moye. He first of all told me about his early career: an accountant for an engineering firm before entering the prison service and in due course moving to Strangeways Prison in Manchester as an assistant governor. He applied for the job in Jersey, was successful in being appointed and arrived in December 2001.

> I was horrified by some of the physical conditions of the place but much impressed by the excellent staff group – very professional and caring with a tremendous can-do attitude. I came just after the Chief Inspector had delivered his report with its 147 recommendations, a lot of them to do with the fabric of the buildings and the estate. The thing is that the 1975 buildings are well past their sell-by date: they don't meet modern standards; the cells are far too small and don't have integral sanitation. Also there has been a huge increase in the prison population in the last two years. But we now have the first new building in the prison for years which is up to modern standards. And tagging – electronic monitoring – was introduced in 2003.
>
> Of course, if there wasn't a drug problem within Jersey, then the level of crime in society would dramatically reduce. We believe that 80% of our prison population is here as the result of drugs – either involved in drug dealing or as a result of acquisitive crime committed to pay for the drug habit that they have.
>
> I trust that my successor will drive forward our redevelopment plan. Not only are we virtually four prisons in one but in Jersey we have to provide every single function; we don't have a local prison, a training prison, an open prison; everybody is lumped in together and sometimes the security measures aren't really appropriate to a particular prisoner.
>
> In many ways, and it's for family reasons, I am sorry to be leaving. I have enjoyed a lot of Jersey's aspects. I cycle and walk a lot. But the one issue I have with the Island is this: its size. I am a city person and I find the smallness of Jersey quite difficult to deal with. The Island has much work to do in appealing to the younger people; the winter in Jersey is a terrible time for youngsters.

Governor Kirby gave me a one and a half hour tour of the prison and kindly made the arrangements for me to talk to two of La Moye's inmates and to one of his prison officers.

Patrick (not his real name) is Irish and has served three years of an 11-

year sentence for drug offences. He has already served time in prisons in Belgium and in the Irish Republic. He told me something of the life at La Moye.

> I find the atmosphere reasonable and the officers easy-going. During the day I do work – making survival blankets. We get access to television which is a help and for recreation it's pool, table tennis and the gym – I go there all the time. I get a visit from my wife each week; she comes for an hour or so. I'm a Catholic and we have a Sister who comes in on a Monday and holds a service. I keep my head above water. I was hard done by with my sentence – Jersey is tough on drugs and it is more than I would have got elsewhere. When I come out I'll be deported and I'll go back to Dublin.

I left Patrick and was escorted to the huge compound which houses the prison's big horticultural enterprise. Here during a tea-break for the inmates I was able to have a chat with Anita (again not her real name) who comes from a Pakistani family in England. She had a moving story to tell.

> I've been here for three months now. I pleaded guilty for drug-running and am awaiting sentence. To be honest, I was involved in difficult circumstances and I didn't know what the consequences would be.
>
> The thing is that I was forced into marriage. I was taken to Pakistan from my home in Slough. I was told that I was going to Dubai on holiday, but my family forced me to the airport and never showed me my air ticket. Once I got to Pakistan my passport was taken away and I was forced into this marriage. I had a gun pointed to my head and a knife at my neck. There was a lot of abuse by the guy I was made to marry – physical, mental and sexual. In the end I could not stand it and escaped in the middle of the night when everyone was asleep. I eventually got to the British High Commission in Islamabad and they then handled it all.
>
> This is what led me into my present troubles. I wanted a divorce but my family wanted me to pay back the money which had been handed over for a dowry. That's how I was pushed into the drug offences.
>
> There's a reasonable atmosphere in the women's wing here. It's crowded but everyone gets on fairly well. I've got a

psychologist and it is good to talk to her. Forced into marriage, I was locked up and have these horrible memories. Now I'm locked away again. I can talk my problems through with her and get some of the anger out as well. Some people do make mistakes and this is a mistake I have made. I wasn't thinking at the time. I have learned from it.

~

Leaving Anita I had the chance to have a word with Officer Tracey Corrigan, a Jersey woman who eight years ago left a job as office manager with an insurance broker in order to take up this post so that she could work with and help those in prison.

The inmates are not in prison to receive punishment; this is their punishment – to have their freedom taken away. If we as staff respect them, hopefully they will respect us back. The good thing about La Moye is this positive aspect – the good relationship between the staff and the prisoners. The negative side is the lack of funding and staffing – to be able to complete your job in the time allocated for it. A lot of us do work in our own time: most evenings I take typing home, doing c.v.s for the girls or printing up information for them from the internet.

The physical conditions in the female wing are poor and the girls do moan about them. I think that if we were like some officers in the UK and treated them like numbers, then I think we would have bad problems. As it is we know our inmates; we know when they are in a bad mood, when they have had an unhappy visit or got p.m.t. We can work around that and with each other.

I do sometimes wonder what I'm doing here when things go wrong, when you have spent your own time doing something for a prisoner, helping with accommodation outside and a job, and then they are back here again in a few weeks. But we have our successes as well as our failures, and I see some of them later in Town and they run up to me and tell me their news.

This prison is like a little village. It is like a family here. When the girls are upset they may get a cuddle; you're not meant to, but when someone is sitting crying their eyes out and telling you their innermost secrets, then it's a help to put an arm round their shoulder and give them a bit of t.l.c.

Desalination plant

Having left the prison, it was not a great distance across a wild heathland and down a steep stepped descent to Jersey's desalination plant. This important element in the Island's infrastructure is set in a deep and fairly forbidding old quarry, La Rosière, and the engineer in charge is Nick Marsh. We first had a chat in his office at the heart of this fairly compact and well-screened industrial site.

We don't operate all the year round, only when we have a shortage of water or the nitrate levels are high and require dilution. The plant is capable of producing 6000 cubic metres a day – that's 6 million litres. The average consumption of the Island in the winter is about 18,000 cubic metres, and that goes up to 24,000 in the summer – mainly because of the use of water in gardens. So you get an idea of how much the desalination plant contributes, when necessary, to the Island's water supply.

When we are operating we have a four-shift day with one person on each shift. Then there's a fitter on day work, and there are myself and my assistant. It's quite an economical operation. The old plant, a distillation operation replaced in 1999, cost £5000 a day for fuel. This one runs on electricity and runs at a total of £2300.

I've worked here for 13 years, and the pluses are that no one bothers me too much. I said to the managing director of Jersey New Waterworks: 'I'm a bit like a fire extinguisher – you're not noticed and nobody bothers you here until you're needed – and then the phone calls start up.'

Then Nick gave me a comprehensive and fascinating tour of his domain. He took me outside and directed my attention to the pumping house on the rocky foreshore below, where the sea intakes are. Then we viewed the quarry pool into which the sea water is pumped. After that come the pre-treatment filters (sand and anthracite), and then the water arrives in a big unit where under great pressure it is filtered through membranes which remove salt, bacteria, viruses and other particles. Forty-five per cent of the sea water converts into fresh water, and the rest is rejected as brine and returned whence it came – to the sea. At the end of it all the fresh water is pumped from here to the Val de la Mare reservoir for blending with natural waters and forwarded for further treatment and distribution to you and me. All extremely interesting!

~

Corbière was now not too far away, but the going on the path was up and down and demanding. Before Jersey's famous landmark, the lighthouse, came in sight, there was another structure claiming my attention, the German-built observation tower, one of the Occupation's most impressive relics and housing Jersey's shipping radio. I rang the bell at its door, described my mission over the intercom, was admitted by the officer on duty and undertook the long spiral climb upwards through various layers of the construction. The effort was rewarded by my arrival in the operations room at the top, with its thrilling, panoramic views out to sea through 270°. Here I was given a warm welcome by Richard Billot. He has an interesting and relevant history: farming for 20 years in St Martin first with his father and then on his own but, with the decline in the Island's traditional agricultural industry, undergoing a career change four years previously.

Our primary job is to co-ordinate search and rescue operations. We are the first line of call from a boat at sea. They will call us for help and we then co-ordinate between the sea-side and the shore-side of things, with the Harbourmaster's backing. There are the lifeboats, the helicopters and so on, and we do all the juggling. Also we get transit reports: a boat leaving St Helier, say, for Granville, will call us up, give the details of the passage and we will log it. And we handle the shipping as well: the ferries call in to us, giving times of arrival, passenger numbers, vehicle figures and so on, and we transmit this information to the Harbour.

We work shifts, covering 24 hours a day, 365 days a year. In the winter it can be a bit quiet unless there's an emergency and then it's pandemonium. In summer it's much busier, mainly with pleasure boats. And one of course has to stay awake during the night shifts. One of my most traumatic experiences was when a fishing boat was lost off Corbière here (and I have fished out of Rozel all my adult life and know the challenges). There was a big search and the bodies were found.

The future of Jersey Radio here is sadly uncertain. It is likely that this operation will be transferred to the Harbour. It will be a great pity; this is such a beautiful place to work from. And here we can keep an eye on what is going on around. Some time ago an elderly couple were cut off by the tide out at the lighthouse and we were able to get the inshore rescue people to ferry them back before hypothermia got to them. And we can also monitor the lighthouse; we can operate it from here. It will be unfortunate if we have to leave. [This has now happened.]

Observation Tower,
Corbière

~

Having descended the stairs from the radio station I was able, at ground level this time, to absorb the rugged scene which Victor Hugo poetically described as 'the herdsman of the waves'. There in front of me was Jersey's famous landmark, the world's first concrete lighthouse, in constant use since 1874 and with 150 steps from the gate to the top. Once upon a time it was manned by four keepers who lived in the cottages on the land side of the causeway; now it is fully mechanised, automatic since 1974. With Richard Billot's account of the two stranded holidaymakers in mind, it was all the more poignant to come across the memorial stone set in the wall at the sea's edge. It reads:

> **Peter Edwin Larbalestier, assistant keeper at the lighthouse, who on the 28th of May, 1946, gave his life in attempting to rescue a visitor cut off by the incoming tide. 'Take heed all ye that pass by!'**

Before moving off in the direction of Petit Port, I had the good fortune to meet Dave Turner who lives at one of the Keepers' Cottages. He was a painter with the Harbours Department for 30 years, has lived here for two decades and for 15 years has had the task of looking after and cleaning the lighthouse. He offered to take me over it and we and his dog set out, the tide being right, across the four hundred yards separating the land from the lighthouse's commanding rock. Then we had the long climb up to the lighthouse itself, passing the shed that houses the back-up generator (if the power fails) and the old machinery, now redundant, for operating the fog-horn, and on up the spiral staircase inside. The place is spick and span and I was firmly told not to put my hands on the well-buffed brass banister rail. At the top the view is unsurpassable, and the lenses and prisms surrounding the light itself are the original fittings, regularly cleaned and dusted by Dave. He also showed me the original paraffin light, gleaming and surprisingly small, a sort of Tilley lamp with its large muslin mantle. After I had taken in the scene we descended and returned to his workshop near the cottages where he told me a bit more about his experiences in this unique spot.

> I love every minute of living here and looking after the light. Of course since it went automatic in 1974 it requires little maintenance, but I go out once a week for three hours doing all the spit and polish, and, with the sea air getting into them, I have to oil all the locks and hinges once a month. Living here at the

Keepers' Cottages, living by the edge of the sea, is a marvellous experience. We have just had big tides of 36/37 feet with a lot of wind with them, and the sea has been boiling and the swells huge. It's fantastic to watch. And then there's the other side to things when it can all be as smooth as a mirror. I do quite a bit of fishing off the rocks here – sea bass, mackerel, plaice and the like; we don't have to go to the Fish Market in Town.

The waters can be very dangerous. Last year we had a man in his sixties who decided to swim out to the lighthouse. There was a lot of shouting and I went into the garden, and here was the man in trouble. Someone got a lifebelt to him and pulled him out before he was taken by the big rip tide.

And on stormy nights I sleep like a log – even through the fog-horn. I say to my wife, 'Is that the fog-horn going?' But it's no use asking her; she sleeps even better than me.

Lighthouse,
Corbière

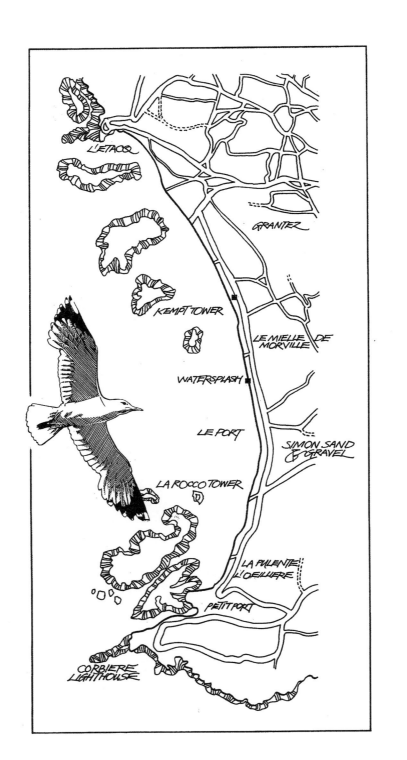

L'ETACQ

GRANTEZ

KEMPT TOWER

LE MIELLE DE
MORVILLE

WATERSPLASH

LE PORT

SIMON SAND
& GRAVEL

LA ROCCO TOWER

LA PULENTE
L'OEILLERE

PETIT PORT

CORBIERE
LIGHTHOUSE

5

Corbière to L'Etacq

I left the lighthouse behind me and turned down the steep hill towards the little known beach of Petit Port, passing on the way a mammoth, fairly new, rather ugly and, for this splendid location, incongruous apartment block. Then I passed several villas facing the sea which would not have seemed out of place in a post-war Esher housing development. (Why generally is the modern housing on the not distant Brittany coast so much more satisfying?) In front of me was the empty and closed Sea Crest Hotel, ripe and ready for demolition. Opposite this former and much missed (at least by me) restaurant I turned up a drive to visit Dr John Renouf who has lived above Petit Port since the Occupation when his family moved here, his father having retired from managing his shop at Maufant.

John Renouf went to school at Victoria College, cycling there and back and clocking up 100 miles a week, was selected for a British Schools Exploring Society expedition to Iceland in 1956, gained a degree in Geology at London University and went on to study for his PhD. In the 1970s he was for seven years the first paid curator at Jersey's museum and then spent 14 years in the advisory service of the States Education Department. I was particularly anxious to learn about his boyhood experience of the shoreline near his home.

> From an early age we explored the coast. I was never interested in boats; for us it was scrambling on the cliffs and swimming. In those days the shore round the south-west was virtually inaccessible but it did not stop the family from going there. We used to scramble through the gorse to the rocks at the sea edge. We would spend whole Sundays down by a little natural bridge on the shore below what is now the prison. Along the length of this coast between Corbière and Beau Port there were caves to explore. We would go into them at low tide and swim into them

if it were high. Very few people know that one of these caves goes in at least 100 metres from the overhang. Later I would explore them all more carefully with regard to their geology. And one of the striking features of that coast in those days were the jackdaws – rooks and jackdaws everywhere. They seem to have gone completely now; perhaps the pesticides have had their sad effect.

Since his retirement from Education in 1993 John Renouf has become ever more absorbed in his geology and archaeology, doing a tremendous amount of work on the matter of stonework in buildings. Before I left I wanted to quiz him on his thoughts about the Island today.

I don't like what has happened to Jersey – too many people and too great an emphasis on money and money-making and this has produced the 'haves' and 'have nots' situation. As to the environment I think that over the years Planning and Environment have done a good job. But I do think that the Town has lacked and needed broad design criteria. I have in mind a book, *The Making of Dutch Cities*, which shows the principles about frontages along canals, with the levels matching but with the details being left to the people. And so you get those fine Dutch townscapes with a riot of detail; but look down the mass and the lines run right.

I would like to see the Plémont holiday camp go; it should be bought and razed. And the coast from L'Etacq to Plémont is worthy of international status with its incredible variety of geology, archaeology and its fine natural environment. Mind you, it was a miracle that St Ouen's Bay was saved from development after the Occupation and the dunes preserved as well. As to Jersey's future I am just conscious of so much pressure, with the creation of a large infrastructure and without the money to sustain it. It is a precarious situation with the finance industry, and I would not like to predict what the future in ten years' time will be.

~

I left John Renouf and crossed the road to a large bungalow which stands above Sea Crest and with a marvellous sea view from its sitting room picture windows of Petit Port below. This is the home of Martha and Julian Bernstein, and I wanted to talk to her about her previous life as a hotelier in partnership with her husband and now as the wife of the ex-hotelier/restaurateur-turned-politician. Martha is a Londoner, educated at the famous St Paul's Girls' School, whose family home was by the Thames boat race course at Barnes Bridge and with a front door painted (I was for personal reasons glad to learn) in rich Oxford blue. She had a busy and successful career in hotel management – including the Grosvenor House and the Strand Palace – before marrying Julian in 1986 and coming to Jersey where he for a number of years had been the manager and subsequently owner of Oaklands Lodge Hotel in Trinity. She combined her early married life with a tutoring post at Highlands College, and then she and Julian decided that they wanted to find somewhere which they could run together.

> Victor Cornaglia used to say to Julian whenever we had a meal at Sea Crest, 'When are you going to buy my restaurant?' And that in January 1990 is what we did. To be fair, the view sold it to us. What is the point of living on an island if you can't see the sea? We had a very challenging start but I was now with Julian an active partner, having a co-operative management scheme and making our decisions together. It was very demanding, with our children born in 1992 and 1996, and after 12 years we made the decision together to come out of the business. The hotel/restaurant had dominated our lives for all these years, the most difficult problems always being to do with staff. And the worst nightmare was inevitably the occasion when the chef told you that he was going. If the chef can't produce the goods, then you might as well pack up and go home.
>
> I saw all sorts of new opportunities for Julian but he was more nervous about the change of direction. Then up came the elections for the States and some of our customers had been politicians. Slowly the penny dropped that this was the way ahead. He made the big leap and much enjoys the busy new life; he is doing things that are interesting, appealing to him and hopefully of value to the Island. He's on Education, Sports and Culture, on Privileges and Procedures and on the Tourism sub-committee. Not only that we have our family life back: we are happier as a family and Daddy is happy.
>
> And my life now? I lived on the tidal Thames and grew up with a body of water outside and on the move. I feel the same here: the passage of the tide and the passage of time. I look up

from my study desk and suddenly the rocks have appeared again. We have this path down to the beach, one of the most underused bits of the Jersey coast. My dogs think that it belongs to them and cannot reason when others want to be there too. It is a stunning spot and we are incredibly lucky.

~

From Petit Port, and having skirted the little bay, I took the path round the headland called L'Oeillère (which means 'the look-out'), with a prehistoric burial chamber up the hill on the right and a huge German gun emplacement on the left. And then the whole noble sweep of St Ouen's Bay came into view, with Rocco Tower out to sea and dominating the middle distance. This 18th century fortification against the French was used by the Germans during the Occupation for target practice, and it was principally the efforts of the Reverend Peter Manton over three decades ago that led to its splendid and important restoration. Behind La Pulente with its pub, restaurant and holiday apartments and rising up to the right are Les Blanches Banques, one of the most extensive sand dune systems in the British Isles, with its Neolithic standing stones and rich flora of orchids, hare's-tail grass, Atlantic clover and the sand crocus. The one man who could tell me more about this five-mile jewel of Jersey's coast was Mike Stentiford, and I went to see him in his peaceful rural Victoria Village home.

Rocco Tower, St Ouen's Bay

Mike is a Devonian, born in Exeter in 1935. After marriage and National Service in the RAF he came with his late first wife to Jersey in 1958 and worked as a commercial artist and engraver with Tubeolight Ltd for over 20 years. During that time he had become active in the Young Ornithologists' Club, a junior group of the RSPB and was also responsible for setting up the Jersey Conservation Volunteers. He then made a career change in 1991 and joined the expanding States Environment Department working as Interpretation Officer. I wanted to learn more about what he had achieved during his time there until his retirement in the year 2000.

One of our greatest challenges was Le Mielle de Morville towards the north end of St Ouen's Bay. It was a very degraded area, with sand excavation and dumping. And the dunes, Les Blanches Banques, had suffered a great deal of people pressure before the notion of conservation had been taken on board. These places have been rescued and transformed.

There have been disappointments too. One of them for me has to be the golf course, with its unnatural bright green impact on what should really be a wild area. And there are the sand pits where, to be fair, the owner is trying hard to encourage wild life. Let us hope that in due course, when the sand excavation ends, it becomes a nature reserve and not a water sports park.

The whole of Les Mielles, St Ouen's Bay, is one of those special places where one can get that bit of wild peace. With so many people in this relatively small island, then these places become both necessary and absolutely priceless. It is not surprising that, when the *JEP* ran a competition asking people for their favourite Island spot, the majority plumped for St Ouen's Bay. When I have had to escort coach parties and they have come round that hairpin bend above La Pulente, there is a great intake of breath as the visitors take in the sheer spread and beauty of what they see revealed before their eyes.

I then asked Mike what his nearly half a century in Jersey had meant to him. What to him was special about the Island?

I have been so fortunate in living and working in such a pleasing environment. I extol Jersey's virtues to both visitors and to locals. A great passion wells up in me. It is the sheer variety of its landscape – so astonishing for an island that is relatively small.

Walk out from my house here and you would be in six different habitats in 20 minutes, be they woodland, beach, reservoir, agricultural land and so on. And there is another thing about Jersey and that is the variety and the talent of the community. There is this community spirit, especially in the country parishes. I discovered that when I started the Conservation Volunteers. We should not knock the Island all the time. There is this great potential: the wealth of societies, clubs and groups representing so many interests; the opportunity for getting off your backside and making a contribution to this wonderful place.

~

A mile or so north of La Pulente I came away from the sea wall, crossed the road, went through a gated entrance, turned right along a dirt track and found myself gazing wide-eyed at the large-scale site with its massive stretch of water of Simon Sand and Gravel Ltd. This big quarry is, it is fair to say, well shielded from the road and has been in existence for near on 100 years since the first shovels were taken to the dunes in this part of the bay. I went looking for Jim Simon, the current member of his family in charge of this considerable undertaking. Jim's home lies behind the quarry and next to Mont à la Brune, a house well known to Islanders at Christmas time when it is extravagantly lit up - to the great financial benefit of the Jersey Hospice, with well in excess of £10,000 in eight or nine years collected from those who have turned up to admire the seasonal and lavish illuminations. Jim was able to tell me much about the family enterprise.

We have gone back through the records and found that the first receipt was in 1909 at the time when building was going on at St Peter's Barracks. A horse and cart delivered a load of sand and the price was six old pence. That's how it started. My great-grandfather had initially bought the land from the Crown in order to graze cattle and was told that he was absolutely mad to do so since the land was so poor.

And we have progressed from shovel and horses and carts. More recently we have used a dredger which is now being superseded by excavators that scoop up the sand with a big arm. We supply every building contractor in the Island – something like 65,000-85,000 tons a year. And we think that there are reserves of about five million tons on the site.

We have just been granted a permit which is due to expire in 2018. The quarry will shut then unless the powers-that-be give us another extension. If we close, then I would like to see a low profile leisure unit here, with the possibility of fishing, sailing, rowing and lots of different things. And of course we are an important bird sanctuary as well.

I think that over the generations my family has been careful in lessening the environmental impact of the quarry. Way back, my forebears resisted it being used as a tip which would have polluted the existing aquifer, and no dumping has ever taken place here. Naturally the authorities always look carefully at any form of extraction and quarrying. We recognise these factors and try and work with them as much as possible.

Now I am handing over to my son and I shall be getting more time for family, going away, bowling and the St Peter's Football Club.

~

It was time for refreshment and I made towards the Jersey Delights ice cream van parked at Le Port (known in my family as 'the bottom of Jubilee') which lies between El Tico and the Watersplash. I found Sonia Lee making the sales from the other side of the van window and she told me that she had been working at this position for about ten years.

The concession has been in the family for 30-odd years. We also do the housing estates and we have a van at Grosnez in the summer. I'm actually engaged to the boss's son. Here it is every day in the summer and the weekends in the winter. And if business is slack and there aren't many customers around, then I have a telly and a stereo which help pass the time.

I like meeting the customers. When things are quiet you get a chance to chat to them. Tourism seems to be slowing down a bit, but we have our local customers as well as the holidaymakers. In the winter I do the housing estates and also the vans are done up for the summer season.

Do I like ice cream? Now you're asking me a question. I'm afraid I love ice cream – except for chocolate. And it can be a temptation. When I started, it was a matter of how many I could eat in a day. I'm not so bad now – perhaps one at the end of the day on my way home. I'm a good advertisement for the product!

~

This area of St Ouen's Bay witnessed the Parliamentary fleet of 1651 attempting a landing, and nearly three hundred years later the Germans considered this the most likely spot for an allied invasion and extended the sea wall and 'anti-tanked' the area with mines and barbed wire.

A couple of hundred yards north of Le Port one comes to what could be considered an architectural incongruity on this coast – The Watersplash, once one of Jersey's most famous and patronised nightspots and recently purchased from the Swanson family by the Seymour Group. Near The Watersplash is a modest beach hut, the only remnant of the many shacks that lined St Ouen's Bay until removed at the start of the Occupation. This hut has been in the ownership of the Oxenden family for many years, and I sought out Jeremy Oxenden to tell me something about the surfing that has been a pastime here since the 1920s when his grandfather Nigel, incidentally the founder of Portelet Holiday Camp, with friends formed the Island Surf Club. Jeremy himself is a professional and self-employed gardener with the freedom to go surfing whenever the conditions are good. Born into this famous surfing family, he has been active in the sport for over 25 years.

After the First World War my grandfather travelled the world – including South Africa, Australia and Hawaii. Along the way he picked up surfing and on his return to the Island and with high-diving friends from the swimming club at Havre des Pas introduced the sport to the Bay, surfing in the summer and repairing the boards in the winter. And this continued, mainly belly-boarding, until 1939. The boards were about five feet long, but there was an Archie Mayne who had an eight-foot board. He would go further out to the big breakers and occasionally succeeded in standing up on it.

My grandfather was then called up as a reservist and continued his surfing in Cornwall during the war. Sadly he died in 1948. In the '50s Harry Swanson brought over some lifeguards from South Africa and they began using wooden stand-up boards – cigarbox, hollow plywood affairs. A new club was formed in 1959; my mother actually went to the inaugural meeting, but it was thought that women wouldn't be any good, being considered not strong enough to carry these heavy boards! As it is the whole family has carried on surfing – my brother, sister and nephew. And my mother these days does kayaking.

The first fibreglass boards came in during the 1960s as did the rubber wetsuits, and this has meant that the sport now goes on through the winter. Today we have all sorts of activity: modern boogie-boarding, short-boarding, knee-boarding, long-boarding, and I must mention surf-kayaking as well.

The surfing at St Ouen's is pretty hard to beat. We may be a bit of a backwater in international terms but we're a busy backwater. And as for me and my family, it is hard to imagine life without surfing. It would be very, very dull. It adds a zest to life. After a great surf you feel good for days. Surfing with your buddies and having a laugh and a joke: nothing better.

~

A few yards north of The Watersplash is the distinctive St Peter's guardhouse and magazine (known as La Caumine à Marie Best after a lady who lived there once the military had gone), white and gleaming and now the property of the National Trust for Jersey, and a bit further on is the increasingly popular Big Vern complex of café and holiday accommodation. The sea wall continues for another few hundred yards to the north of this, with Kempt Tower looming in front and, across the road to the east, St Ouen's Pond or, more correctly, La Mare au Seigneur, considered the largest stretch of natural water in the Channel Islands. One person with a special claim to knowledge of this area and indeed the whole of Les Mielles is Richard Le Sueur who spent his childhood in the house designed by his architect father, Richard, overlooking the Bay and whose mother, Frances, devoted so much of her life to the study of the area's botany. Richard is himself an architect, educated at Victoria College and then at Cambridge, returning to the Island to continue the practice of his profession in 1993.

> My father built his St Ouen house in 1957, having bought a slice of the hillside. His interest in Les Mielles went back further. My mother had grown up in Carlisle and her interest in botany had been kindled by holidays on the Solway Firth. She came to the Island to teach Mathematics at Jersey College for Girls. That was in 1948, and my parents met while bird-watching at the back of St Ouen's Pond a few months later.
>
> As a boy I did not greatly relish the sand aspect of the beach but liked the ice creams from what was then called Pro Tem, now Cutty Sark. At the age of 11 or 12 I became very interested in bird-ringing and the activities of the Société's ornithology section and used to go freshwater fishing in the north canal.
>
> And what is special about St Ouen's Bay? It is the openness. Compare it with the east of the Island with its little wooded coves. Here, however, drive down the Five Mile road and look – no hedges, no banks, no mounds. We are fortunate that the Bay is as it is. I won't name names, but there are some quite difficult people around who could threaten this environment. Forty or fifty years ago it was the Swansons who had a scheme to turn the Bay into another Costa Brava with 20-storey hotels going up. It was a time of great plans to destroy the area and great plans to save it, and fortunately the preservationists won.
>
> And think of the early '70s when there would be a great pall of smoke over Les Mielles. It was the Island's dumping ground and there was the burning of refuse and summer plagues of flies. The great improvement from that point of view is mirrored by the landscaping improvements too – there used to be telegraph and electricity poles all along the Five Mile Road, forming a timber canyon of wires. They have now all gone.
>
> I believe that the golf course was a substantial mistake; it is the artificiality of it that offends. And the sand pit and its area of water is alien to the Bay. It cannot be filled in; it is the aquifer for the Island and even inert waste of concrete and brick would be

polluting. So it will remain as an open body of water, and in the future there is the danger of unsuitable leisure activities being developed there.

As to the future of St Ouen's Bay, hopefully it will continue as it is, becoming ever more popular for people able to appreciate the natural world and enjoying themselves in a non-mechanised, non-technical way. For me it is a very special place. Politicians come and go, and new political phases and fads come and go. Eternal vigilance is required; sustainability is the buzzword of new planning systems, and we must be on our guard against any threats to this worthy objective.

~

I now continued north along the sea wall by Le Mielle de Morville, now a pleasant area for the public to roam and explore, with the sand pits and rubbish dumps now fortunately no longer. Along this stretch of the Bay The Barge Aground, an Art Deco Noah's Ark, cannot fail to catch the attention; the Scouts and Guides moved a few years ago across the road to a handsome, low wooden building and there are plans afoot for their former property to be renovated and available for holiday lets. The top end of the Five Mile Road has its less than edifying facilities for the tourists and their shopping needs. I passed quickly by and made my way along the wall to Le Grand Etacquerel, the promontory and northernmost point of St Ouen's Bay, dominated by a big German gun emplacement which is now the headquarters of Faulkner Fisheries. I wandered in and was ushered into a wooden shed at the side of this concrete fortress. Here presiding over all his fish operations was Sean Faulkner, ready to tell me about himself, his business and also his frustrations. He was brought up at L'Etacq just across the road, and his father and grandfather had both been fruit and vegetable merchants. Thwarted by eye problems from pursuing a career in the Royal Navy, he became a purser on cruise ships and in due course returned to the Island in 1980. He applied to the States for permission to convert this derelict German relic of the Occupation into shellfish *viviers,* and this has been his base ever since as his export, wholesale and retail fish business expanded.

When I took over the building I had to break down the concrete to get in. It was a hell of a mess and I had to get rid of all the old bottles and cans and mattress springs before I could start and build in the tanks. I bought a place in the Fish Market in the mid-'80s and I also operate out of Guernsey, Alderney, the south of England and in France. We send shell fish to France from all these various sources. We have a boat based in Guernsey and articulated trucks doing the European traffic.

I conduct all these operations from this little shed, and over the years I have had a constant battle with the Island planners who refuse to have anything to do with any kind of improvements which I would like to make here. We have a portaloo and one basin, and my employees lack the facilities to change or shower.

The powers-that-be kill enterprise. That's the way the Island is going. I sadly see zero expansion. I have no wish to damage a beautiful bay, but this is an existing building put up by the Germans. We are a business that has proved very useful to the local community. If we were helped, then we would do better business and pay more taxes. Businesses like mine are throttled while a few which seem to become monopolies are supported. We are making use of this otherwise derelict place out here at L'Etacq; we export; we supply the hotels and restaurants; people come for the retail trade here and in the Fish Market. I like to think that we are doing a service to Jersey and I wish that the b****y authorities would see a bit of daylight and give me some help. It's all very negative.

Before I left, Sean, now calm and controlled, gave me a tour of his small, damp, little empire, with its busy staff in their less than adequate working conditions preparing and gutting fish in and around the brimming, flowing tanks with their rich hauls of mussels, lobsters and crabs. An interesting place and, in the Michelin phrase, 'worth a detour'.

~

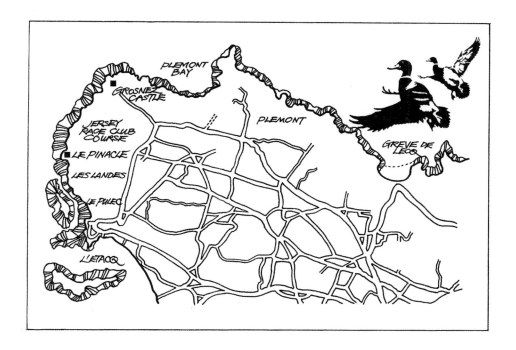

6

L'Etacq to Grève de Lecq

Having left Sean Faulkner's *viviers*, I walked up the road past Le Pulec, known to some as 'the stinky cove', found the coast path going off on the left and climbed the flight of steps onto the wild, open plateau of Les Landes. This is the largest area of continuous heathland in Jersey and with much to occupy the attention: Le Pinacle (Jersey's answer to The Old Man of Hoy), the model aircraft flying activities, the rifle range and its butts which were in use until the 1950s, another impressive German observation tower similar to that at Corbière, the mile-long Jersey Race Club course, the ruined Grosnez Castle at the top end and the views to the north of the other Channel Islands – even Alderney on a clear day. The person who could put some of this into perspective was Dr Ralph Nichols and I sought him out in his home above St Peter's Valley.

Ralph Nichols was born in the Wirral, went to school there and then progressed to the University of Wales at Aberystwyth where he read Geography, Geology and Economics. He gained his PhD in Geology in 1961 and then spent five years in Australia, helping to make some of the original geological maps of its central regions. He also had two years in Saskatchewan looking for oil and gas under the prairies before coming to Jersey, the home of his parents, in 1968. He then spent a career teaching in the Island, for many years at Grainville until his retirement in 1995. He is virtually a Renaissance figure: a wide range of subjects taught, an interest in and knowledge of Jersey French, holder of a PSV driving licence, instructor in scuba diving and dinghy sailing, still a hockey player, and much more. It was worth meeting him and I quizzed him on the geological significance of this part of the coastline.

Let's start at L'Etacq. There is a geological reason for this big headland at the north of the bay. The headland is the more resistant rocks, and L'Etacq marks the change-over from the softer rocks that have eroded faster and formed the bay to the harder rocks – the granite. At L'Etacq you can see where the granite has intruded into the softer shales of the bay area. There are veins and dykes of granitic rock that have been forced into the grey shales and stand out as bars of granitic material. There are a couple of mineral veins as well – a silver and a lead and zinc vein, now largely covered up but mined in the 1800s. You can take a fork and dig the seaweed out at Le Pulec and see it. The cove is a beautiful site for teaching geology.

Now go down to Le Pinacle. This is fascinating archeologically and geologically. It's incredible: you have got the intrusion, one of about eight sills. Those intruded vertically are called dykes, and one at Le Pinacle has been used by Neolithic people and during the later Copper Age for making implements. Le Pinacle itself is actually an ancient sea stack, possibly used as a natural menhir – standing stone. Granite is normally jointed in three directions and forms cuboid blocks. There are other sets of joints at different angles, and marine and weather erosion occur among the joint places and eventually isolate the more compact rock leaving it as a marine stack.

Ralph Nichols had more to say about the coast stretching from Grosnez

Le Pinacle

to Plémont, Sorel and Ronez, and this was too good a chance to miss, despite these places lying ahead of me, and I quizzed him further.

> This coastline is quite different from that of the west and south of the Island: narrow inlets and no large bays. And Plémont itself provides a good example as to the causes of inlets. You have master joints – the biggest fractures in the rocks – and you have also got vertical intrusive structures – the dykes. There is one just to the east of the Plémont steps. You can see that the rocks are softer, made of iron and magnesium and silicates; they are more easily weathered and eroded than the granite. So you get marine erosion from the base and weather erosion from the top, and the inlets are formed at the sites where the master joints and the intrusion of the dykes occur. You can see the same thing further east at Ile Agois as well.

Before I left Ralph I wanted to ask him more generally about Jersey which has been his home for nearing 40 years during a hard-working life.

I have a deep love of the Island, its landscape and topography and the valleys, the bays and the headlands. It has been so clean and unpolluted, with no industry to do environmental damage (I don't count the quarries which I regard as natural and which, to me at least, blend in). And there are the people, and I have always been fascinated by the French links.

The more I learned about the geology, the greater became my knowledge of the Island's botany, zoology and marine life. And as to a final thought, I hope that there will be no further loss of the buildings that constitute Jersey's heritage. Think of people abroad; think of France and the crowds that swarm to Dinan, Sarlat or Cordes. Where, however, is the old part of Jersey and of St Helier? Perhaps St Aubin High Street and its environs alone retain that particular charm. Bring back the cobbles! The sad fact is that we are becoming like any other place and, if people do not have something special to come here for, they will go to the cheapest and sunniest resorts, and it won't be Jersey.

~

I strode on north across Les Landes, leaving the now derelict firing range on my right and with the tall German tower coming into view before me. On the right I could now see the white fencing of the race course, and I knew who would be able to tell me in general about the history of horse racing in Jersey and in particular about this popular track. I went in to Town to visit chartered accountant David Picot.

David was born into a Trinity farming family, attended Victoria College and broke with family tradition by going into the offices of Alex Picot (a distant and relatively remote ancestor) to serve his articles. He has been a rider from his earliest years, his first pony coming in 1960 from a circus that was seeking a winter home for it. Horses have been his main hobby ever since – the drag hunt, show-jumping and, in his earlier days, racing at Les Landes.

For 20 or so years I was an amateur jockey, with about 15 wins in all: six or seven meetings a year, and just one win a year if I was lucky. Things started to change in the late '70s when professional jockeys would come in for the day. It's now 95% pro, and the odd amateur may get a ride occasionally. I'm a Steward of the Channel Islands Racing and Hunt Club; we're the body, equivalent to the Jockey Club in the UK, that controls the sport in Jersey.

Racing at Les Landes goes back to 1961, but horse racing in the Island goes back to the earlier years of the 19th century. In 1832 there was a two-day meeting on the St Aubin's beach, and in the mid-century the Jersey Race Club functioned on Gorey Common. There's a painting by Ouless showing horse racing there. And for 40 or 50 years in the first half of the last century the sport centred on Les Quennevais – where the Sports Centre is today.

But, as I say, we have been at Les Landes since 1961. For the last 20 or more years we have had eight or nine meetings a year. There are four major trainers in the Island and perhaps about 45 horses in training, with 35 of them running at each meeting. And with the professional jockeys it's true that the standard of racing has steadily improved.

As a spectator sport horse racing in Jersey has taken the place of football. We have between 1200 and 2500 at each meeting; 15-20000 people in all going to Les Landes during the year. The track is superb, with a watering system and as good as any of the smaller courses in the UK. What is less than perfect are the facilities for the public: for example, no plumbed toilets. There are current plans for a clubhouse but, speaking personally, I would like to see a stand, tastefully designed and appropriate for the special environment of this part of the Island, which would incorporate the amenities which the public requires.

We continue to need sponsorship; keeping the actual track and fencing up to standard and our permanent groundsman cost money. Racing is very much part of Island life and a good tourist attraction as well. It has been part of the Jersey scene for 170 years and I see no reason why it will not continue to prosper in this fine and wild north-west location.

~

I soon arrived at the top end of Les Landes and what is left – not much – of Grosnez Castle. The guide books are divided about 'Grosnez'. Does it mean 'big nose' or 'big cape'? But there seems to be common ground about its history: probably early 14th century; probably not so much a castle but more a refuge for the inhabitants of the area taking shelter with their livestock from the marauding French. It is thought that by the 16th century the place was a ruin and, lacking a water supply, not ideal for withstanding sieges. A stroll through the remaining arch and down to the light below on the cliff side was worthwhile before I continued my walk, this time to the east rather than the north, towards Plémont.

Grosnez Castle

Now Plémont, actually Grève au Lanchon, the sand eel beach, must surely rank as one of the Island's most stunning bays, with its wonderful sand, its white-flecked breakers and its many caves, one of which is improbably reputed to stretch inland to Portinfer. The only fly in the ointment is the holiday camp on its eastern headland, too sadly evident as one strides along the cliff path and, at the time of writing, deserted and decaying and with the fate of the site – back to nature or a housing estate – undecided. I knew whom I wanted to meet here, the young owners for several years of the Plémont Beach Café, and I turned down the concrete road to this welcoming establishment above the steps to the beach which Darren and Emma Amy by their hard and skilled work have made so deservedly popular both with locals and tourists alike.

Darren is a scion of the family that for generations has owned Amy and Son, gents' outfitters in Queen Street, was educated at De La Salle and later at Bournemouth University , studying hotel and catering, and then returned to the Island. Emma was born in Guernsey, travelled the world with her mother and came to Jersey at the age of ten. She met Darren when he was running a restaurant in Town, and both of them went to England for a time, working for Starbucks. They came back to the Island and within three weeks had a child, sold their house in England, purchased a home here and took over the Plémont café with a long lease from the States. Both of them have much to say about tourism and the art of being successful. Darren kicked off first:

> We have got busier every year for four years. There may not be as many tourists around, but it is what you do to attract them. If you are a bad business, then it's easy to blame the Island for not having tourists. But if you work at it, you'll get them. Look around: it's the bad businesses that close and the good ones that flourish.

Emma added this:

> Outlets have had to pull their socks up. Take the cafés. They have raised their standards, and there is this café culture; the whole family can be involved. Also there isn't the pressure, with drink and drive as well, to have a bottle of wine. And you can bring the children. It's a much more relaxed way of eating. I do all the cooking and Darren does front of house. In the summer I need to be here early at 6 a.m. to get the cakes and scones on.

Darren chipped in enthusiastically:

> I never get bored with this wonderful place. We spend our time being surrounded by people in awe of the area. The fact that Plémont is difficult to get to is part of its charm. And I look out every morning at this view and think that's how it looked hundreds of years ago and how it will always be. As to the holiday camp, they must do something urgently. From my own point of view I would flatten it and return the area to the wild. But perhaps a compromise with 20 or 30 houses or a golf course may be reached. At present it is a symbol of our dying tourist industry: here's one building which used to have 300 tourists staying there, and now we're falling apart.

I then asked Darren and Emma about future plans and Emma's response was:

Darren is the most ambitious person I have ever known. But I hope that his ambitions will lie dormant for a year or two, that we have time to breathe and take stock of what we have done in the last few years. We're probably a bit more tired than we think: we open seven days a week from 1 April until the end of October and at weekends all the year round.

And Darren added:

For the time being this is right for us. We went to New Zealand for our honeymoon and absolutely loved it. We thought it could be paradise with its opportunities and cheap properties. But as we flew back we were sure that you couldn't compare it to Jersey for lifestyle. We decided that for the time being our future was here. When we took over the café it was very run down, but I just knew that it had potential. Everyone at the time said we were daft: Plémont will be very quiet; the holiday camp is going; we think you're mad. But people didn't realise how busy we would get. That was Emma's and my challenge, and to find something else like this will be difficult.

~

Replete with coffee and cake, I left Darren and Emma and called in on the Plémont lifeguard in his hut situated on the café's roof. Nick Woolnough was just starting his seventh season in Jersey and, with a grey day outside and no swimmers in the water, he had the time and the opportunity to tell me about his early years.

I've lived in Sydney all my life and went to school and university there, doing a Bachelor of Arts degree at Macquarrie. Then I started travelling the world and for several years I have been lifeguarding at home and here in Jersey. I like the Island a lot – a fantastic place to spend the summer.

The lifeguards usually do three days at St Ouen's Bay and then a day here at Plémont and a day at St Brelade's. There's a particular danger here, with the high tide covering the beach and people getting stranded on the rocks. I rescued several last year who had got trapped. And there was a particularly hairy day at St Ouen's three or four years ago when, with a strong rip tide, we did a total of 48 rescues.

We have our gold medallions in lifeguarding, first aid certificates and advanced resuscitation training. We've actually got a defibrillator here, and they're pretty foolproof these days, virtually telling you what to do.

The lifeguards rent a place in town, and in my spare time there's swimming, surfing and the gym. I like Jersey a lot, with everything so close and easy to get to. You can ride round on a bike. As to whether I shall be coming back, I'm not sure. Physiotherapy is an option for the future, but at the moment I'm content with an agreeable summer season before me.

~

I left Nick and climbed the steps to the holiday camp fence, took the cliff path above the bay's eastern headland, the Tête de Plémont, and started my switchback progress towards Grève de Lecq. This is two miles of sheer delight, with the route going inland at Lecq Farm along the lanes before reaching the path that affords stunning views below of one of the Island's most popular beaches.

As I descended towards Grève de Lecq there was a house on the left, high above the beach and with panoramic views towards Sark and the closer Paternosters reef. I rang the bell in order to meet its owner, Paul Sands. Paul grew up in Kings Lynn, just eight miles from the sea, and as a child came to know well the bleak north Norfolk coast. After attending the local grammar school he went to Birmingham University and took a good degree in manufacturing sciences before joining Cadbury Schweppes as a management trainee. Years later he was personnel director of one of the Cadbury subsidiaries and, with colleagues, effected what was then the biggest management buyout in UK business history. Three and a half years later, the company was sold on and Paul, having considered Canada and Australia, decided to come to Jersey.

I always wanted to live by the sea, and my wish was fulfilled here – this stunning beauty and the sweeping views along the north coast and out to sea. And the crowds here in the summer are no bother – there is a buzz of happiness from the beach, with the sound of the waves louder than any noise made by people. It's a great family beach; it doesn't intrude in any way; but I rarely go in for a dip; much as I like the sea it has to be around 20 degrees before I am tempted.

Grève de Lecq has recently had this good quality housing development, but I have a sneaking nostalgia for Caesar's Palace, however hideous its premises were. I had always pooh-poohed the idea of cabaret, but the shows were of the highest standard and my visitors and I used to get some first-rate entertainment there before it closed for good.

I have been in Jersey since 1992 and for the last four years I have been active as a Samaritan. I have the luxury of a fairly flexible use of time; I wanted to get involved in some form of charitable work; and the Samaritans is 'hands-on' rather than sitting round a committee table.

Paul now runs his own investment company and, with his long previous experience in industry, I wanted to ask him about Jersey, its system of government and what he sees as the future of the Island as a finance centre.

When I came here in the early '90s I thought how fortunate Jersey was – no worries about the Island's income, and all the States had to do was to spend it. Looking back, perhaps Jersey did not read the signs soon enough; good economic husbandry was required for the future. One of the factors in holding back remedial action has surely been the nature of the Island's government – 53 independent members of the States and no political parties. And it seems to me that the most vociferous of the politicians want to be in opposition. I believe that something like the Clothier reforms is essential; indeed Clothier probably doesn't go far enough. And another danger is that we gain a Clothier structure of government but that we lack the quality of people to take on the most important ministerial posts. Many of them seem to want to get on these scrutiny committees because they want to be in opposition. But they don't realise that scrutiny is not opposition; scrutiny will be there to check that the ministers are enacting the policies, and that is different.

Jersey is a very small place and perhaps, with the *JEP*, local television and local radio, we have too much news. With everybody knowing everyone else in a small island it is difficult for our 53 politicians to say 'no'.

As to the future of Jersey's finance industry I think that, in order for the continuance of its prosperity, it is the cost of doing things which is the problem – in other words, high inflation. There needs to be a more realistic approach to wages and salaries. Population as such is not a problem: population will ebb and flow according to the success of the Island. Agriculture has run out of steam; tourism would require huge investment and hotels on all the best beaches. In fact the finance industry is a fantastically low user of resources – no industrial sites, no factories, no pollution. But there is nothing magical about Jersey as a finance centre; there's no one out there who is going to come to our aid. The industry is now well regulated and enjoys a good reputation, and what we need to do is to bring our cost of service down and then the future should be bright.

~

Grève de Lecq, once an old smuggling harbour, is surely one of the Island's most popular and delightful spots, with its beach crowded in the summer, its cafés and pubs (one of which, the Moulin de Lecq, has a working waterwheel used in the Occupation to generate electricity for German searchlights), its attractive new 'pastiche' housing, its little jetty and, on its eastern flank, its imposing Barracks. The person who could tell me more about all this and much else was Charles Alluto. Since 1999 Charles has been Chief Executive of the National Trust for Jersey, which owns and administers the Barracks,

Officers' Quarters, Grève de Lecq Barracks

and lives in the Officers' Quarters there. He first outlined for me the history of the Barracks, built in 1810 because of the threat from Napoleon and thus becoming yet another of Grève de Lecq's fortifications in addition to the round tower, unfortunately located in the middle of what is now the car park, and Le Câtel, the little fort above the bay on the east side, built in the 1780s to house 15 soldiers and with three gun emplacements.

> The Barracks housed 150 soldiers and sit becomingly in terms of the whole impressive site. Walk across to the pier on the west of the bay, look across and see how enhancing is this complex of buildings. And I am fortunate to live here, summer and winter, and step outside my door to be welcomed by the sight and sound of the bay, with the Paternosters and Sark beyond. An ever-changing scene.
>
> The National Trust has plans to revitalise and update this important possession of ours, and I can see the Barracks acting as a sort of gateway to Jersey's fine north coast.

Before moving on I took the opportunity to ask Charles about the National Trust for Jersey, its current work and his ideas for its future development.

> My view is that the National Trust is an undervalued asset to the Island. I don't think that people fully appreciate what the Trust's potential is. It needs to be supported more heavily and more vocally. Jersey is under considerable threat and we have the capacity to be a strong counter-balance against dangerous pressures. As an organisation I think that we should try and make our sites more accessible, and then we can engage with the public more successfully than has been the case in the past. And protection of the north coast is surely a priority; here is Jersey at its most unspoilt. Plémont and the holiday camp is a major issue here, and I hope that the Trust will campaign heavily to prevent the headland being re-developed.
>
> Our recent acquisition in Town of 16 New Street is also important: St Helier continues to change dramatically and listed buildings are being knocked down regularly.
>
> So there it is: we have got to get the public behind the National Trust for Jersey, generate more support and get people to see that it is not just one other organisation but theirs for safeguarding the Island's heritage.

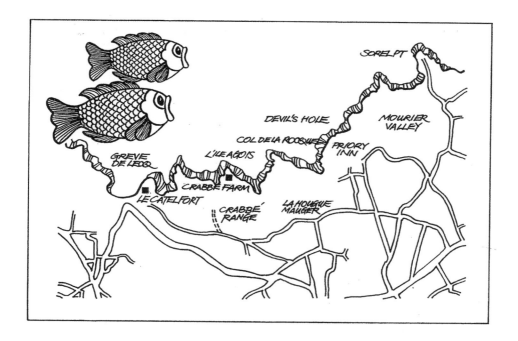

7

Grève de Lecq to Sorel Point

I now turned up the steep lane behind the Barracks, after 100 yards passed the track to Le Câtel Fort and continued up the one-in-four gradient. On the left near the top is Jersey's answer to Silbury Hill, namely the Castel de Lecq, an Iron Age construction which seems to attract little attention in the guidebooks, yet another fortified position but from a somewhat earlier age. As the road flattened, the Crabbé ranges lay on my left, and after half a mile I turned north towards the sea and came upon Crabbé Farm, superbly restored some years ago and the home of Bernie Baldwin, Crabbé's range warden.

Bernie is a long-time military man, having joined the army as a boy soldier in 1956, and rose to being a regimental sergeant-major in the Royal Engineers before taking a commission in 1981. By 1987 he was Major Baldwin and the officer in charge of the Island's newly formed Territorial Army squadron. In 1990 he also took on responsibility for the ranges, retired from his army post in 2001, is now a health and safety consultant and continues with his duties at Crabbé. I sought him out in his office near the airport.

> The ranges have been at Crabbé since 1860, have been rebuilt at least twice and include facilities for Jersey Pistol Club, the main gallery range, a small-bore outdoor range and a clay pigeon range. We also have the Jersey archery here. I love my job, managing the ranges; it's just my line. And I'm also secretary of the St Mary Rifle Club which has been going for over 100 years.
>
> On the site there is also the explosive compound where explosives for Ronez, Granite Products and the Police bomb disposal are stored. I've signed a waiver that I won't sue the States if the whole thing blows up!
>
> Of course my wife and I have lived with the now defunct Crabbé compost site across the road. Fortunately with the west wind the smell, such as it was, blew away from us. I thought that the major problem with it was the large size of the vehicles and the small size of the lanes.
>
> I have been in Jersey now for nearly two decades and have always thought it fantastic. You fly back, get off the plane and at once feel more relaxed; the pace of life is better than on the mainland. Good restaurants, friendliness, drivers waving you on; it's marvellous. Of course we all moan – that's one of the small things, with everybody knowing everyone else. But if I won the lottery I wouldn't want to move. It's Jersey for me.

~

Leaving Crabbé Farm and the derelict compost site behind me, I strode on towards the sea, coming past a field beside the coast path which had been given in 2003 to the National Trust for Jersey by John Perrée. He is from a well-known St Mary farming family and I knew that a chat with him at Plaisance, next to St Mary's parish church, would be rewarding. He told me that he had first farmed at The Oaks, St Peter, until moving to one of his father's farms, which is still his home, in 1945. After 1969 he had become a successful agricultural contractor. He told me first about his gift to the Trust.

This was a field that had belonged to my father who farmed at La Forêt where I and my brothers Frank and Henry grew up. In my youth half of this field was never cultivated; the east side was full of beautiful gorse five or six feet high, and some of it was cut into long bundles, tied with wire and brought back home by horse and cart as fuel for the bakehouse. Then later I farmed it. We had good Breton labour – men born with a scythe in their hands – and the bracken would be stacked and used as cow litter. I then grew rye there for a couple of years and this conditioned the soil for potatoes. Later I let it to a succession of tenants, and it continued to yield potatoes until the States agricultural people considered that it was too stony. Lying fallow, ragwort caught hold, and the States Farm officials ordered us to get rid of it. Not an easy task. So I decided to give the field into the safe keeping of the National Trust, and they were delighted to take ownership of these fine coastal vergees. My uncle had given The Elms to the Trust, and other Perrées have also in the past been generous. I was glad to be able to carry on the family tradition.

I was not going to leave John Perrée without allowing him to reminisce about the Occupation and to consider the state of Island agriculture today.

We were five years under the Germans. We still farmed but were very much regulated by them. Even the milk was controlled by inspectors. But some of us were on the ball. Along with an inspector would be a German checking him. To get milk for ourselves should have been easy, but not so simple with an inspector looking on and writing out the quantities as you milked the cow. So the dodge was this: when they came and you were doing the milking, you would declare that those two cows were dry. The moment the inspector was gone those two cows got milked.

As to agriculture now, it is all very sad, with the potato, our national crop, at the mercy of the supermarkets. Now we are seeing numbers of our fields completely abandoned because of the low prices for the crop. Large numbers of potato growers will have to give up. What will it all be like in 50 years' time? With exported semen, the export trade in Jersey cows is dead, and the Island herd is getting too small for viability. A vet said to me some time ago, 'One day the only place you will see a Jersey cow is in the zoo.' I shudder to think what our island will be like in years to come. Will all fields be either for people's horses or converted to golf courses?

~

Leaving the ranges and the disbanded compost site behind me, I strode east along the cliff path. A bit of grit found its way into one of my trainers. Was it one of my parents-in-law? This is where we had scattered their ashes. In a quarter of a mile or so I was above Crabbé Bay and there was the Ile Agois. For more information I turned to an extract from the 1979 Annual Bulletin of the Société Jersiaise. Here was a paper by Margaret Finlaison and Philip Holdsworth presenting the facts:

> The Ile Agois is a tidal stack...Although at one time a part of the headland which encloses Crabbé Bay on its eastern side, it is now separated from the mainland by a narrow gorge 12m wide. The island rises to a height of 76m above sea level and has an area of 417 square m...Access to Ile Agois is difficult and may be gained at low tide by descending the coastal cliff, crossing the rocky beach and climbing the south-west face.

Having scaled the face 30 years before, I put aside the temptation (which was not strong) to repeat the exercise and instead sought out Margaret Finlaison herself at the Société's archaeological headquarters at Hougue Bie. Her work on Ile Agois had confirmed that this fascinating location had had three periods of use or occupation: the early Iron Age, the pre-Roman Iron Age and the early medieval period. There is also an attractive idea that in the seventh or eighth century it was an eremitic monastery.

Margaret told me something of her earlier life, coming to Jersey with her doctor husband in 1960 and then steadily gaining archaeological experience, with much practical work in St Helier where she and colleagues carried out four major excavations, digging in all 96 test trenches and, in the course of this, discovering the lay-out and extent of the medieval town. She told me more about her Ile Agois work.

> The island was examined earlier in the last century and the conclusion was that it was an Iron Age settlement. For our excavation we spent quite a few weeks camping on the site, with the fire brigade rigging up a breeches buoy for the supply of our

Ile Agois

food and water. It was springtime and the seagulls, with their fledglings and upset by our presence, were attacking us all the time.

We were examining what seemed to be the remains of huts – huts piled on others like a beehive. I invented a tradition that the person discovering the most interesting finds should supply a bottle of champagne, and my husband sent over a bottle in the breeches buoy. Of course the island was joined to the mainland at one time and the bridge probably disappeared – collapsed – in the 10th century or later.

Margaret enthuses about the other sites of great interest in Jersey. Le Pinacle is one and another is of course the col at Mont Orgueil. The latter is particularly important – early Neolithic, 4600 BC or thereabouts. She spends her time trying to stop tent pegs being driven in, paths and steps being created and surfaces levelled. And she is also firm in her opposition to recent proposals for the castle itself.

The last thing you do is to put lavatories in a building like this. And they will go on disturbing the ground with pipes and cables and so on – without any proper archaeological research being done first. It's a crime. And there never was a Tudor great hall in the castle, and the powers that be just don't want to know.

The most urgent need is for the States to appoint a paid archaeological officer with a unit working with him or her. Such a person should be doing rescue work in Town. The rest of Europe has such people; Guernsey has had one since 1976. But not here. Our contemporaries in Britain are appalled at the way archaeological research here has been sidelined. As it is all the sites in the countryside are ignored and fieldwork in the Town is done in an ad hoc way – always a rearguard action. It is an appalling situation, a complete blot. And all the time they talk about 'heritage' but they don't know anything about it or how to look after it. Basic ignorance!

~

I now cheated slightly. I turned my back on the sea and walked 300 yards up the bridle track to La Hougue Mauger, which is the site of a dolmen with some of its large stones incorporated into the garden wall. I wanted to meet

Daniel Wimberley, hirer-out of bicycles and tireless campaigner for worthy causes. He is the son of a former Jersey Director of Education, went to Victoria College and on from there to read Linguistics at the University of York. There he organised Fasts for World Justice and then for a number of years lived in communities, latterly in Norwich where half of the members consisted of those with learning difficulties.

When we came back to Jersey I worked initially for Mencap. I was with them for over two years, investigating projects in the UK and eventually handing on the work to a States department. Since 1991 I have been running my cycle hire business, a significant tourism development – getting away from the 'bucket and spade' variety. The establishment of the cycle network through the Island was a huge step forward. I am known for my strong views about cycle helmets and question the rationality of those who insist on their use. It is disturbing and galling when Headway, a charity whose aim is to minimise brain injuries, goes on all the time about helmets, helmets, helmets. They seem to be anti-cycling and it is irrational. Helmets don't help and can harm. Some kinds of cycling require helmets, but it is not a blanket solution. It makes the cyclist into the victim.

Christian Aid – I am Chairman in Jersey – is a continuing commitment. I have always been bothered about inequality. Like other similar charities it is not primarily about fund-raising; the fund-raising is a tool for involving people, bringing people into the movement, getting them concerned about the issues of sustainability, third world debt and trade justice. This awareness is growing and growing among young people. When we put cereal into our breakfast bowls, when we eat a banana or orange, we are connected. I talk in schools and describe the difference between a fair trade banana and a conventional one. It is a knock-out. And the questions come: how can it be as bad as you are telling us?

I pressed Daniel to comment on some of Jersey's current political issues and concerns. It was interesting that in response he first mentioned the parishes.

The parishes have a huge potential that has not been fully tapped. They could be better at being communities. And in fact the parish meetings are undemocratic, with perhaps 60 parish worthies having control. Others don't go because the meetings are dull, and the 60 then have their way. The person who becomes Constable comes from the 60. It is a kind of closed shop, part of the alienation process that puts people off voting.

I am not sure about a party system for Jersey; it can't be invented. But it would have an impact on young people. Parties, if they want younger members, will go out and get them. And more needs to be done with regard to freedom of information. The idea that you get better government behind closed doors is ludicrous and unjustifiable.

I am an incurable optimist. Perhaps it is because I live in St Mary and can walk the lanes. Incidentally, the lanes are getting wider. They are the prettiest roads; they are part of our heritage (and I have to admit that the more beautiful Jersey is, the more bikes I can hire out). But the tractors, the heavy lorries and the four-wheel drives are wearing down the sides. The banks get steeper, there are more mud slides and erosion, and more trees fall down. It is a case of nothing being done until it is too late.

~

With my conscience properly pricked I made my way back to the cliff path, turned east and soon reached Col de la Rocque, described by Balleine in his *A History of the Island of Jersey* as 'the finest viewpoint anywhere on the Island'. It would be hard to disagree: Sorel Point to the east, Grève de Lecq just visible to the west, in the north-west Guernsey and Sark, and the French coast ever closer. It was a delightful half-mile stroll from here to the Priory Inn at Devil's Hole where the landlord is the very likeable and popular Martin Walbridge. Martin came to Jersey on holiday in 1974 and has been here ever since. He worked in various licensed premises in Town, did a season at Fort Regent and has been 'mine host' at the Priory Inn since 1989. Refreshed by an 11 a.m. coffee on the house, I began by quizzing him about the building itself.

It's 13th century. That fireplace over there is protected and the tourelle, that granite winding staircase, is one of the oldest in the Island. This where we are sitting was a farm, and the original priory with its 13th century wall is across the road. It was always known as Devil's Bay here because of the smuggling – a nice distance from St Helier and not too far from the French coast.

In 1831 a French coaster went down on the Paternoster reef and a seaman who swam ashore fell off the cliffs, broke his neck and died. So the farmer from here, a Mr Arthur, got a boat and rowed out and saved the people off the ship. Now the actual figurehead of the coaster was a devil's head and that was washed up through the cliff tunnel into the Devil's Hole. After a time, arms and legs were carved onto it. The original got burnt in the late 1950s by what was thought were the Ku Klux Klan, but it turned out to be three boys up the road with a sheet over their heads. Of course it's been a tourist attraction for more than 100 years and the Victorians came here in horse-drawn wagons to view the cave and the devil.

It's different now. I am in a position here to feel the pulse of the tourist trade. It's dying, and it's had no money invested in it. We haven't enough tourist attractions in the Island. Nobody wants to walk for four days solid; the zoo's a half-day thing as are the Living Legend and the War Tunnels. If the weather's bad, there's too little choice.

And what keeps me going? It's the people; the financial rewards of a 15-16 hour day aren't great. We're a family pub, with a mix of tourists and locals. But the summer trade is not what it was when I started here. The drink/drive has had something to do with it, and I fear that the country pubs won't be able to carry on for ever.

I'd like to be able to turn the clock back and have Jersey as it was when I first came. It used to be very friendly and a good place to be. Now it's just full of a lot of greedy people. And in my opinion there's little leadership and it doesn't seem to know where it is going.

~

I felt compelled to cheer myself up after these gloomy prognostications. It was a fine morning and it was at least 25 years since I had been down to Devil's Hole itself, that impressive cave with the arch and the sea rushing in at high water. Its proper name, incidentally, is Le Creux de Vis – a screw hole or vice. I scooted down the asphalt path, took in this famous north coast feature and, rather less quickly, made my way back up the hill to the pub car park. I then picked up the coast path again, crossed grass close-cropped by rabbits and descended to Mourier Valley with its reservoir and pumping station, part of the public water supply system. I climbed up again, coming in half a mile to one of the 12 parish millennium stones - modern megaliths, the initiative of Philip Le Brocq when he was President of the Société Jersiaise - at Sorel Point. Here is another marvellous *point de vue*, with reefs visible to left and right: to the west our now familiar Paternosters and to the east the Dirouilles and Ecrehos. It is also worth one's while to slip below the headland, Jersey's most northerly point, and inspect (from the outside) the lighthouse that lies beneath it.

Lighthouse at Sorel Point

~

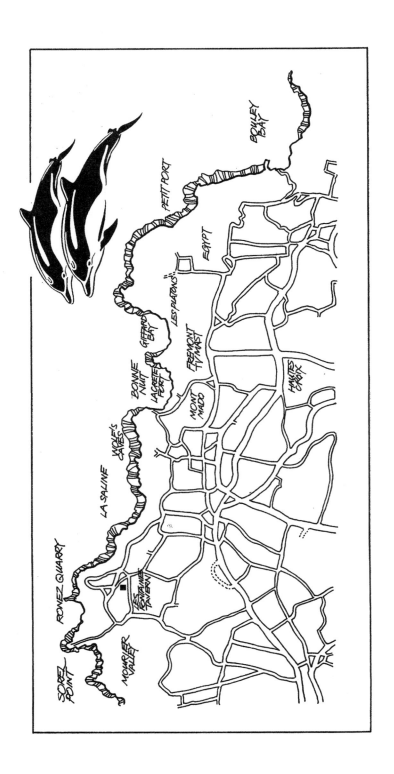

8

Sorel Point to Bouley Bay

I turned my back on the sea and walked up the road from Sorel Point. An amazing sight opened up on the left – Ronez Quarry, a remarkable and massive gouging out of the rock. I had to find out more about this huge excavation and went in search of Paul Cragg who for 15 years has been the quarry-master here. He first told me something of the quarry's early history.

> Quarrying started at Ronez in the late 19th century, and quite a lot of stone was exported in those days. Go to the Thames Embankment and you will see Ronez stone used on the banks there to cut erosion from the barge traffic. In those days there was no hard rock in the south of England and it was more efficient and economical to ship it direct from here by coasters and then up the Thames.
>
> During the Occupation the Germans worked the quarry, and there was a railway from here that distributed the aggregate via the German rail network through the Island to the sites being fortified. Nowadays nothing is exported. As to the future we haven't yet had the vigorous debate in the States as to the future of quarrying in Jersey
>
> I think we're rather good at keeping the blasting quiet. We don't want to upset our neighbours; we have strict guidelines and the quarry is a nice horseshoe-shaped bowl that looks out to sea and cuts down any noise generated by blasting and crushing.
>
> You may be interested in one or two statistics. Ronez has in all 140 people employed in the Island, and within the quarry there are 16 drillers, blasters, machinery plant operators and maintenance staff. Currently we extract about 150,000 tons of crushed stone per year. Sometimes it's a bit more, sometimes a

bit less; it is related to the state of the construction industry. Our working depth currently is 110 metres. Across the horseshoe it measures about 300 metres. And some of our workings are below sea level, with a satisfactory bridge of rock left in place to keep the tide out.

Ronez Quarry

There's never a dull moment working here. Is it dangerous? We hopefully keep on top of that and, in this age of health and safety, try to take a lead in these matters. And everything in the operation is done by machine so that the workforce are largely isolated and protected from the most hazardous risks. No breaking of rocks with sledge-hammers these days; it's all done by modern technology.

~

It was now time to tackle the mile of pavement along the Route du Nord but, before that, refreshment was at hand at Les Fontaines Tavern. Joan Stevens in her *Old Jersey Houses* points out that few people see the south façade of what was an ancient farmhouse, and she speaks enthusiastically of the round arch 'composed of ten stones, the supernumerary being an extra small one to the right of the keystone, a curious aberration and perhaps a miscalculation on the part of the mason'. Inside, this busy pub-cum-restaurant is a mix, not without its charm, of the ancient and the phoney, and the fireplace in the main room gets a good Joan Stevens mention. I have to declare an interest here: this is the hostelry where those of us who ring the bells at St John's church come for our beer after the Wednesday practice night. On this occasion it was the morning and I was soon in conversation with the manageress, Helen O'Gorman. She told me something about herself and her work at Les Fontaines.

> I was born in Limerick City, went to primary and secondary school there and then came straight into the trade, working first in a local pub and then in a new Limerick hotel. I met a girl there and we decided to come to Jersey for the summer. This was in 1995 and I have been here ever since. My first job was at the Goose on the Green at Beaumont – just for the summer - but when the season ended I decided to stay. I did my college training – the British Institute of Inn-keeping – and some relief managing for Randalls, wanting to take over my own pub. And I have been at Les Fontaines since the year 2000.

Les Fontaines Tavern

> It's a beautiful pub; everyone remarks on that. It's got atmosphere and all sorts come through the door – visitors, families, young toddlers, locals. And various groups have their regular nights: not only you ringers, but the Triumph Club and

the moto-cross and go-kart people. We do very well, with the takings in the summer being big, and surviving through the winter with our Jersey customers.

What brought me to the Island? In fact our next-door neighbours in Limerick came here on honeymoon, and that's when I first heard of Jersey. It was to be either Jersey or the Isle of Man for me, and I came here. I get home three or so times a year and family have been over on holiday. The Island is a great place – friendly, everyone knowing everyone. As to the future I'm going to stay here, please God.

~

Leaving Les Fontaines (until the following Wednesday's bell-ringing evening) I crossed the road to the car park opposite and read the stone which is set in the middle of it. It reads:

> **THIS ROAD IS DEDICATED**
> **TO THE**
> **MEN AND WOMEN OF JERSEY**
> **WHO SUFFERED IN THE WORLD WAR**
> **1939 1945**

This commemorative plaque records the fact that much of the Route du Nord was built during the Occupation by 3000 men and women without work. It was one of the schemes devised by the States to provide employment.

The stroll along the road's pavement is not the most exciting stretch of the north coast. Half-way along you pass the St John's parish cross, erected in 2000 to mark the millennium (we shall leave aside the controversy of that year concerning millennium stones v. millennium crosses), and one soon reaches La Saline quarry where access through steel gates and along a gravelled track takes one once again onto the cliff path.

Above to the right loomed the huge Frémont TV mast. I was frustrated in my first attempts to find out more about this massive feature that dominates the Island's northern skyline and, having skipped round the locked gate and rung the bell of the buildings at the mast's base, I encountered the engineer on duty who seemed anxious about national security and refused to answer my questions. I had to discover a different source of information and tracked down ex-States Deputy Jimmy Johns who before retirement had been a radio engineer at Frémont and at Les Platons, the aerial complex a little further along the coast. Born in Chichester, he joined the BBC after service in the RAF, arriving in the Island in 1960 and joining the team looking after the Les Platons transmission station. I first quizzed him about his job there and about the more prominent Frémont site.

> When I first worked at Les Platons it was simply a transmitter for BBC1 black and white television. It was a two-shift job and one sat at a desk monitoring the signal coming in from two aerials, selecting which of the two signals was the better. It was boring as hell actually! Later, colour TV arrived and then the BBC co-shared the Frémont site which had originally been the ITV mast. Later Les Platons was expanded to accommodate VHF radio and another mast was added there for that purpose. There's also another block at Les Platons to house an emergency back-up diesel generator and this is meant to be nuclear blast-proof to ensure the operation of the system in such an emergency. Both Frémont and Les Platons are now in private ownership, with the engineers employed by the respective companies.

I was also anxious to find out more from Jimmy about his political involvement which had begun in the 1960s when the Communist Norman Le Brocq, leading light in the Jersey Democratic Movement

Frémont Mast

came knocking at his door asking for a donation to support him as a member of the States.

> I was radicalised by the Suez war in 1956 and became a political animal then. When I came to Jersey I was appalled by its feudal nature, the role of the Constables, the honorary system and the like. All this was absolute anathema to me. By the end of the '60s, as a young ingénu I became involved in the JDM and for years attempted to get elected to the States. But party politics was not Jersey's way, and that was what the JDM was about.
>
> Eventually in 1993 I was elected for the St Helier No.2 district, having taken the decision earlier to drop the JDM connection. I had tried hard to re-establish myself as something different, getting rid of the old radical image, becoming vice-chairman of the Royal Air Force Association, taking over the organisation of the air display and so on. Yes, it was an exercise in manipulation and perhaps the ego was to the fore, but it succeeded and I was elected, having retired from the BBC after 36 years and being utterly fed up with all that.
>
> I was in the States for six years until losing my seat to Jennifer Bridge (who was everything I was not: a new broom, young and female). For three of those years I was President of Harbours and Airport, resigning in a blaze of controversy in 1998. Both the airport and the marina developments had overspends, but I am proud of what was achieved with both. The fact that the airport overspent by only £2m was a miracle. The marina went £7m over budget, and it all descended on my head again. It looked horrendous but there were a number of mitigating factors. I think that we got off lightly with this overspend, but the general perception was that we had wasted public money.

I then asked Jimmy Johns about his thoughts concerning Jersey today, a few years on since he ceased from being an active politician.

> I think that Clothier and ministerial government is along the right lines, but I worry that there may be a reaction to it all when it starts to work. And change for a small offshore community is tricky. This is understandable when you consider Jersey and its history, having over the centuries to face French threats and having to fend for itself. That's the underlying pulse of the Island

community – clinging to the Crown, a sense of frugality and so on. What I am into now, besides bowls, is the population thing. It may be considered a right-wing point of view - and I am not a right-wing sort of person - but it seems to me to be completely counter-productive if there are too many people living here. I eventually got the States to debate this in my final time there. I sought agreement for the setting of an upper limit as a top strategic priority, with everything else being of secondary importance. The proposition was lost by six votes – 15 for and 21 against. But I am glad and proud that I raised the matter.

I am an optimist about the Island: Jersey has always looked after itself and triumphed over adversity because of the sheer pig-headedness of its people. I say that without being prejudicial: pig-headed people always survive and in the process they are not always nice people to know. But they do have those admirable qualities of tenacity, of single-mindedness, of not giving the outside world a chance to do them down. In other words, if the finance industry went tomorrow, they would find some other way of goddamn earning a living.

~

Resuming the path at La Saline I now endured one of the steepest flights of steps on the whole coast in order to reach what was once the Wolf's Caves public house but which in recent years has been developed as the Abundant Life Christian Centre. (Incidentally the cave itself is only accessible from the sea, and the books tell me that it is 350ft long, 60ft high and 50ft wide). Andrew de Gruchy is the pastor of this new church and I called on him and his wife Serena in their adjacent flat.

Andrew is a St Mary boy who did his secondary schooling at de la Salle and then learned a trade as a joiner, first with the family firm and then on his own. Serena was five years behind him at St Mary's primary school, went on to Jersey College for Girls and then worked in a bank. I quizzed Andrew about the discovery of his vocation.

As a boy I went with the family for many years to Bethlehem chapel in St Mary. God was at work in my life at that time, but the first real trigger in embracing the whole Christian faith came in 1986 when I returned from an African overseas aid trip and found that a friend had become a Christian and started talking to me about Jesus. Then a couple of years later, walking back home after a night's playing cards for money and passing the Jersey Aero Club premises, God said to me, 'What are you doing with your life?' Later I was at an evening service at Bethlehem and the Minister's words persuaded me to commit my life to Jesus. Ever since, I have been discovering what life is about and that God has a purpose for all of us.

Serena told me a similar story:

I was brought up going to Bethesda with my family. I had always believed but it was only a Sunday thing. But at the age of 15 I became a Christian and this started affecting the whole of my life.

Abundant Life Christian Centre, Wolf's Caves

Andrew then recounted further parts of his life story: his marriage to Serena in 1993 and their skiing holiday in France with a Christian travel group which led to an invitation to join the firm. They rented out their house, sold the joinery business and moved to England. Then followed two years with Oakhill

Expeditions, travelling a lot and experiencing the excitement of people holidaying with the company and converting and becoming Christians. From 1998 to 2000 they both did a course at Belfast Bible College, and this was followed by the invitation to Andrew to become pastor of Tesson chapel. Two years on, the premises were proving too small and the opportunity of Wolf's Caves opened up.

The pub was built in 1971-2 and closed in 2000. I was walking on the coast path and came across it, all boarded up. I then rang Le Masurier's, the owners, and made enquiries. In due course we reached an agreement and rented the property. It all needed a lot of work, much airing and painting, and God has blown our expectations out of the water. People have come and shared the vision; our numbers have doubled and lives have been changed. We named the church carefully – Abundant Life. It comes from John, chapter X: 'I have come that you may have life and have it in abundance'.

We came under a lot of pressure at the start. Just after we had been here two weeks, my father died tragically. But God was ever-faithful in being our comfort and strength. We could still know joy and hope. God pulled us together tightly in those days, and he has brought good from that tragedy.

The Itex walk, with 800 to 1,000 people, came through the other week. We gave them coffee and cakes and didn't charge for it; we wanted to bless the walkers for what they were doing, for supporting charities and being involved. We had a baptism last week – four people and full immersion in the sea at Bonne Nuit. It was a day of torrential rain and wind. But at the time of the baptism, as we left here, the rain stopped and the winds dropped. In amongst the boats the water was calm.

It brings light to my heart as a pastor to see people's lives changed. There is a real nervousness about the Island's future, particularly when we think of the financial climate. But if our lives are built in the Lord, no matter the circumstances, there's a stability, there's a hope beyond anything this world can offer. And here we are seeing and experiencing the joy of people recognising this in their lives. It is really, really encouraging.

~

Leaving Andrew and Serena and their evangelical centre, with his wonderfully encouraging words ringing in my somewhat more sceptical ears, I returned to the path and soon reached a fine viewpoint, with the little harbour of Bonne Nuit below me. I reached the road, turned left and made my way to the granite jetty built in 1872. This is the finishing point for the annual Sark to Jersey rowing race, and a plaque on the harbour wall commemorates this. It reads as follows:

THIS PLAQUE WAS UNVEILED BY
CHAY BLYTH C.B.E., B.E.M.
ON
27th JULY 1991
TO COMMEMORATE THE SILVER JUBILEE
-
THE RACE WAS INSPIRED BY THE ACHIEVEMENT IN 1966
OF CHAY BLYTH AND JOHN RIDGEWAY
WHO ROWED THE ATLANTIC IN 92 DAYS

By the sign I came across three men looking out to sea over the harbour wall towards the not-too-distant French coast and had a chat with them. They were sailing companions who had come across the day before from St Peter Port to the St Helier marina and were now doing a little overland sight-seeing along the north coast. Bruce Lister is a semi-retired company director from Dublin; David Braithwaite lives in Chester and retired some years ago to devote himself to sailing, with a yacht berthed at Dartmouth; Richard Armspach has lived in France for 12 years and still works – in computers. Bruce had been to Jersey 30 years ago and made this comment to me:

> The Island seems much more modern now – an awful lot of buildings which I wouldn't have recognised from my previous visits. But this part of Jersey on the north coast is unchanged – the pink granite and the slate roofs. But St Helier – far busier and loads more traffic.

David had never been to Jersey before and his first impressions were promising. He hadn't known what to expect, had heard all sorts of stories and thought it a very pretty island which had been sympathetically developed over the years. 'Very pleasant; lovely beaches, nice people, good places to eat' – nor was he in the pay of the Tourism department. Richard had been to Jersey once before when he was aged seven ('a long time ago').

I have fond childhood memories of the beaches and always remember how clean the place was. It still is. The flowers everywhere make a big impression. Jersey always has the air of being clean, and the people are as friendly as I recall.

~

I made my farewells to these three contented customers who were planning to sail away in the morning to Alderney and Cherbourg. I walked along the length of the jetty, rounded the wall at the end and met two fishermen, with rods and line over the railings, sunning themselves comfortably on the bench. I announced my purpose, and the younger of the two said, 'Robin, you've already recorded me for your last book [*Speaking of Jersey*].' He removed his sunglasses and revealed himself as Chris Le Quesne, former Head Boy of Victoria College. Next to him was his father, Peter, who is the joint owner of The Green Olive restaurant in Anley Street, off the Esplanade in Town. Peter told me about the fishing:

> I've only taken it up in the last year or so. It's mostly at Grève de Lecq and we're not very good. The normal catch is nothing, but the occasional rock fish makes a good soup. I've been here to Bonne Nuit once or twice before. It's good to sit in the sun and possibly catch bream. We use ragworm or frozen squid as bait but may change to feathers for mackerel or bass.
>
> By the way, The Green Olive is going well since you had a meal there: good food, a good chef, mostly local business with a strong lunchtime trade. We don't advertise a lot; it's all done by word of mouth. And it's a change from the hotel industry and then the motor trade which I was in beforehand.

I then turned to Chris and caught up with his news:

> I've now just finished my second year at Leeds reading English and am back for the summer and hoping to get a bar job to tide me over. It's good to come back and relax after being stuck in cold, grey, dismal (at times) Leeds. As to my fishing career I have to confess that it is limited and embarrassing. Yes, we did once catch enough to make a couple of rounds of fish soup – unexpectedly tasty, thanks to Dad. And we have been out occasionally on a boat from the marina in Town for slightly more

serious sport.

Incidentally after university I'm hoping to go travelling, and then it may be journalism, law or teaching. But all very ad hoc at the moment!

~

It was time for a cup of coffee with a large piece of walnut cake and I turned back from the harbour wall and made my way across to the Beach Café which has been owned and run by Pete and Anita Pallot for well over two decades. I managed to get Anita to leave the scone-making for a few minutes and tell me about the business.

Over more than 20 years we've seen all the ups and downs of the tourist trade. I think the '80s were our busiest time, but since then the tourists have fallen off but the local custom has grown. Twenty years ago lots of people would arrive by bus and we had a big trade in breakfasts and coffees. That's all gone, but we do have our regulars, retired people who call themselves the Bugger All To Do Club who meet here every morning at 9.30. You should go along and introduce yourself to them; they're over there.

We open from a week before Easter until after the October half-term holiday. We like to go away for a couple of months then, and then there's the maintenance to do on the café for the next season. Pete and I used to do all the cooking but we've now got a chef who does a lot of it. We still do the scones and the coffee and walnut cake and can always step in when needed.

Bonne Nuit has a special charm – a nice little fishing harbour with people relaxing and watching the fishing boats coming and going. Years ago we had the bucket-and-spade brigade; now we have groups of walkers. We shall never get back to where we once were, with cheap flights, package holidays and reliable weather elsewhere. You can't compete with that, but we still get people coming back year after year – old faithfuls – and we're still a popular place.

Another 21 years? Watch this space. We're getting older and have enjoyed it all, made lots of friends and would miss it a lot if we didn't have the café.

~

Fisherman's hut, Bonne Nuit

I made my way from the harbour café back to the main road, turned left and climbed the hill until I reached and followed the track to the Cheval Roc Hotel, incidentally the site of an 18th century barracks. A few hundred yards on I arrived at La Crête Point, lying between Bonne Nuit Bay and Giffard Bay. This headland was fortified by the States of Jersey in 1813, and the squat building on it is now the summer 'bungalow' of the Lieutenant-Governor. One can read all about the Fort's history in an article published by the Société Jersiaise entitled A RESPECTABLE LITTLE WORK, THE STORY OF LA CRETE FORT, but I did one better and went to see and talk to the Lieutenant-Governor's aide-de-camp, Colonel Charles Woodrow. He met me in the offices that lie behind Government House on St Saviour's Hill and, rather daringly I thought, took me for our chat into the handsomely panelled study of His Excellency himself (who must have been away). Charles grew up in Kent, went to Wellington College and was commissioned into the Grenadier Guards in 1965. He had a rich and varied army career, which included commanding his regiment's second battalion and gaining a Military Cross and an OBE. He left the army in 1991 on a Friday and started work in Jersey as ADC on the following Monday. I first asked him about La Crête Fort and the use made of it by the Lieutenant-Governor.

> Government House took the fort over in or around 1970. I have served under three governors and they have all valued it. We use it for some official entertaining, taking ministers and senior officials from Whitehall there when they are visiting us. Some of our staff go there and organisations such as the scouts and the

orienteers have had permission to organise events there. Also
the Victoria Club holds its annual barbecue at La Crête.

La Crête Fort

Sitting comfortably in my leather armchair, I wanted to find out from Colonel
Woodrow a bit more about his role as ADC.

I am something of a jack of all trades. I am responsible for the
efficient running of Government House and its household and
also the efficient running of the office. It's not just 'piss-ups and
parties' as some people think. They do not realise that all official
communications between the UK government and the States pass
through this office. And we have an important role in immigration,
with the Governor ultimately responsible for all such matters –
deportations, refusing people naturalisation and so on. We manage
all the many engagements of the Governor and the Governor's
wife. Don't forget: they are patrons of 100-plus organisations.
We entertain through the house over 3000 people a year, and
1018 came to this year's Queen's Birthday Reception, a record
of all records. I'm also responsible for the arranging of visits to
the Island by royalty, ambassadors and so on, and honours and
awards is another part of the job. I have to see that all this goes
smoothly.

How do I see the role of the Lieutenant-Governor in the life
of the Island? It is one of importance, but we have to tread
carefully – we are not the insular authority. But the Governor is
a valued shoulder to cry on and can be approached by the
politicians and the Bailiff. He can bring to all this an independent

view, just a bit outside the system and not affected by local prejudice and that sort of thing. The Governor's knowledge of the Island is probably better than most people's simply because we may be at one time in the Royal Court and then we are visiting the tiddly-winks society, or we are at the Rugby club, the hospice or mixing with the fishing people. Our actual finger on the pulse is as good as anybody's.

It will be interesting and a little different perhaps when Jersey acquires its First Minister, and that may have an effect on protocol. He or she will be more than just the president of a particular States committee.

I have now been here a number of years and it has been a fantastic experience. I didn't realise at first how hard the work would be. The parties and the entertaining are part of the job, but there is so much more. During my time there have been many occasions when the Governor has had to play an important role and make serious decisions. Anybody who thinks that the Lieutenant-Governor is merely a figurehead wants to come up here and see what his important and true responsibilities really are.

~

I left La Crête Fort and took the lower path round the rim of Giffard Bay (also known as Dead Man's Bay, from the shape of rocks at the eastern end and their resemblance to a recumbent figure), eventually climbing steeply to the viewpoint of La Belle Hougue. From here it is a mile or so along this beautiful and exhilarating section of the north coast path to Petit Port and, in the trees, the little cottage called Wolf's Lair. This was where British and French commandos in an abortive raid landed in 1943, and a memorial tablet, surrounded by tired Flanders poppy wreaths, commemorates the raid:

**THIS MEMORIAL IS DEDICATED TO
THE BRITISH AND FRENCH COMMANDOS
WHO TOOK PART IN
OPERATION HARDTACK 28
ON
25TH AND 26TH DECEMBER 1943.
THE COMMANDING OFFICER
CAPTAIN P.A. AYTON
WAS FATALLY WOUNDED DURING THE RAID**

Memorial at
Wolf's Lair

Another steep climb, another viewpoint with the French coast ever nearer, a wooded inland diversion, and Bouley Bay, with its little pier built in 1828 both for the oyster industry and also for the inevitable defence from our Gallic neighbours, lay below. A stepped descent brought me to the road and past the Water's Edge Hotel to the harbour. Bouley Bay has its Dive Centre, its fishermen and its hill climb. I went to find out more.

At the Dive Centre below the hotel I got talking to Jimmy O'Connor. He is a Geordie who came to Jersey in 1976 as a painter and decorator for six months, met his wife, sadly now deceased, and has been here ever since. Diving was at first a hobby but, with his wife running the café next door, he became manager for Jimmy Webster of the Dive Centre. He filled me in.

> Jimmy Webster started it all, bringing diving to Jersey and opening the Centre in 1948. It's reputed to have been the first such in Europe. Nowadays my involvement is in renting the workshop at the Centre and doing the servicing of the diving equipment, the cylinder testing and so on. And I am a boat skipper. That's mine over there by the harbour wall. I take out charters – people wanting to do the wrecks. It's nice for British divers to dive for German wrecks sunk by British ships rather than the other way round.
>
> There are a lot of wrecks in these waters, many sunk during

the war. Most of the local wrecks are a mile or two offshore. But last Saturday we were nine miles off Corbière, diving to the *Princess Ena*, a passenger ship that caught fire and sank in 1935. People also dive in the bay here, seeing flat fish – plaice, sole and the rest. In fact the business is booming, with the diving usually going on from Easter to the end of September.

As to myself I have no regrets about coming to Jersey those years ago. It's a beautiful place, but I may emigrate to New Zealand. I've a friend with a dive centre there, and I may go in with him or start up my own business. The Island has been good to me; it's just the politicians that have ruined it.

In fairness to him, Jimmy did follow this last remark with a loud laugh. Before I left I asked him whether he knew Ben Lumsden who in my headmastering days in York had been one of my sixth formers. He not only knew him but had sold him the boat which Ben and Chris Goold use for their scallop diving. It was the signal for me to contact my former pupil and have a chat and a pint of beer in order to catch up.

~

It was a warm summer's lunchtime, the draught bitter tasted good, and Ben had generously brought his old headmaster a gift - 15 of the juiciest and freshest scallops. After St Peter's, York, he had gone to Southampton University, studying archaeology (including a module in underwater archaeology). For three years after that he was with Abacus in the finance industry, had travelled for the inside of a year in Australia and then decided to start scalloping.

> I had been diving since I was about 14 when on holiday. I decided that I wanted to do something other than office work, and we make a reasonable living diving from March until the end of September when the restaurants become less busy and demand for scallops drops off.

I like eating scallops but know nothing about them. Ben told me more.

> They're hermaphrodites, cold water shellfish which are found from the north of Scotland down to the Channel Islands and the north coast of France. With Jersey's big tides, clean water and

higher water temperatures, there are a lot of nutrients, and the scallops grow faster and bigger here. They swim by opening up their shells and propelling themselves along; they open up the top shell, warn off predators and feed with the tide. It takes them about three years to become a marketable size. Are they hard to find? You have to know what you are looking for, where to find them; it's experience really.

Unlike the dredgers that scrape up everything on the bottom, we dive around the reefs – the Paternosters and the Ecrehos are good – and with the diving you are picking up scallops one at a time.

We work as a pair, with one of us on the boat and the other diving and attached to a buoy that marks where we are and where we are drifting in the tide. Each of us uses a couple of tanks of air, perhaps about two hours each. With the journeys out and back and with the process at the end of taking the meat out of the shells, a trip is roughly six or seven hours. And our average haul is probably about 250 scallops each. We sell these good hand-dived scallops direct to the top restaurants, among them Green Island and Bistro Frère.

And when the diving season is over I find other work. One year it was standing in for the curator of archaeology at the Jersey Heritage Trust; another year it was a bank job. A varied and happy life in a friendly island!

~

Before resuming my walk towards Rozel I wanted to hear about the Bouley Bay hill climb, and a man who knows more than most about these events and with a family history of participation in them is Peter Le Gallais. Peter was educated at Victoria College and spent three years in England, two as an accountancy articled clerk and one working at Harrods before returning in 1960 to Jersey and the family firm in Bath Street. He is the sixth generation in the company founded in 1825 by his great-great-great-grandfather who was a cabinet-maker. On the death of his father, Frank, in 1982 he became Chairman, and since then the firm has diversified with part of its St Helier buildings let for offices and with commercial property acquired in England as an investment on full repairing leases. Having picked his business brains, I turned to the matter of the hill climb.

It all started in the early '30s and my father was involved in it from the beginning. It's run by the Jersey Motor Cycle and Light Car Club (they also organise the sand-racing down at St Ouen) which, incidentally, is one of the oldest motor clubs in the British Isles, and there are four events at Bouley Bay a year. And who race? There are three categories of cars – saloon, sports and racing cars – and motor-cycles and side-cars as well.

My father held the record for years, and my involvement started around the age of 10 when he would drive his car – very fast - to Bouley Bay and I would be in the racing car being towed behind it, doing all the steering and braking. It couldn't have been legal; if it were today we'd have been arrested. But it was wonderful as a young boy to have that task and privilege.

I started racing when I came back to Jersey, with an Austin Healey Sprite with a super-charger on it. Then I built with my father a little 'special' based on an enlarged go-kart but with suspension. That had a Triumph 500 twin motor-cycle engine with a super-charger. I've actually got it downstairs in the workshop, having bought it back a few years ago, and I'm going to rebuild it. The thing is that I sold it when I married; we couldn't afford a honeymoon, so the £200 for it paid for three weeks in Villefranche on the proceeds.

So I gave it all up for many years and only started again in the mid-'80s. I bought a Caterham and then in due course a Pilbeam, and with this car I got the local record – 40.21 seconds – and it still stands. By then it was all beginning to get a bit serious and in the end I wondered whether I was enjoying it any more and stopped. But they are to introduce a historic class and, who knows, I may get the little 'special' out again one day and have another go.

It's not without its dangers. Over the years, but thankfully not recently, there have been two fatalities, but the element of danger of course is an ingredient in the thrill of the sport. And I must say that it is regarded as one of the very best hill climbs in the British Isles.

I couldn't leave Peter Le Gallais, with his long experience of business in Jersey and with his many-generations family tradition, without asking him his views on the Island's future well-being. Was he an optimist or a pessimist?

It is true that with the finance industry we have become terribly reliant on one source of income and, partly as a result, the States have been so extravagant. That is a worry. But somehow Jersey always seems to weather the storm. Other industries have in the past come and gone and I am optimistic enough to believe that at the end of the day we shall prosper. Things may change, but the delights of this lovely island will remain. And, dare I say it, if in the future a few people left, then Jersey might be even nicer.

Bouley Bay

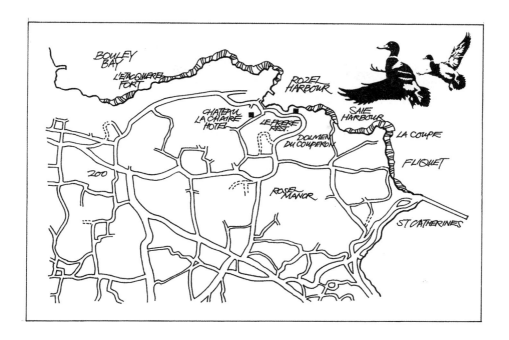

9

Bouley Bay to St Catherine's

Few worries about the future of Jersey bothered me as I set out on a fine summer morning along the coast path towards Rozel. I threaded my way round the back of the Water's Edge Hotel and quickly got into my stride with one of the steepest stepped ascents of the whole route. Blood, toil, tears and sweat were amply compensated for by the beauty of these high cliffs, known as Les Tombelènes, with their August bracken and heather freshened by recent rain. At the eastern end of the bay I passed *Son de la Mer*, a modern house that must surely command the most stunning view of any Island residence (how was planning permission granted for its construction here, or is it on the site of an older dwelling?), and then descended to the locked and barred ruins of L'Etacquerel Fort, yet another Island defence against the French – who seemed to me, casting an eye in their direction, to be extremely close.

A mile on and I was at the Tour de Rozel, Jersey's most north-easterly point, and sank onto a bench bearing a sad inscription:

> **IN MEMORY OF ROY SPENCER AND TERRY RENNELL**
> **WHO LOST THEIR LIVES AT SEA NEAR WHITE ROCK**
> **27TH JULY 2003**

Unfortunately the headland here to the west of Rozel is a no-go area for walkers – the property of the recently restored Rozel Fort and with no public access. (Would the owner's peace and security be at all compromised by a path skirting the house at a low level?) I took to the lane and soon found myself above the pretty harbour, built in 1829 to shelter the oyster boats that operated out of Rozel. Down at sea level I headed straight for The Hungry Man café, the comfort of a mug of coffee and a chat with Katie Blampied.

Rozel Harbour

Katie was born in the Midlands and has been in Jersey for three decades, first in hotels, then working at The Hungry Man and, ten years ago, taking over on his retirement from the previous owner. She is a popular figure on the Rozel scene and has her finger on the pulse of life around the harbour.

Our customers are a mix of locals and holidaymakers, but the tourists are dropping off these days – perhaps a 30% decline in the last five years. I know most of the people around here. I live in Town but have been coming here since my children were small – for 25 years. It's home from home to me. What's special about Rozel? It's a beautiful place – a favourite spot, small and cosy.

I asked Katie for her thoughts about the Island.

It's a lovely place to live and so safe. But Jersey has its problems. There's poverty and unemployment. It's not just good news, is it? There's a big divide with all the poorer people. And tourism needs tackling: the cost of flights and making it easier for people to come. Jersey's got all the beauty; it's just the price to get here. You can't rely on the weather, so we need to lower the prices to attract the holidaymakers. That's the main complaint I get. But the Island should be left alone; don't spoil it. You know, they're trying to build decking here over this corner of the harbour. I'm not in favour of it. Leave places natural; that's what I think.

I'll be retiring from here one day, but Jersey's special, whatever the problems, and I shall never leave.

~

Suitably refreshed, I stumbled across the shingle beach, avoiding the ducks and geese that congregate here, towards the Beau Couperon Hotel and fell into conversation with two holiday-makers in their cycling gear sitting and taking in the scene. They were Jeremy and Ruth Owen-Hughes, on holiday with their three children who were playing somewhat nearer the water. They told me that they came from Yarm in North Yorkshire and were staying at the Rozel camping park up the hill. Jeremy is a technology manager in the chemical industry at Billingham and Ruth teaches technology at a Yarm secondary school. Ruth told me that they had two and a half days of their stay left, and I asked her what had been their impressions of Jersey during this their first visit to the Island.

When I was a little girl we never went abroad, and my friend came here on holiday and she came back very brown. I thought that Jersey must be very exotic. And then, although this sounds very cheesy, there was *Bergerac* and it has always been somewhere we wanted to come to. So here we are.

Jeremy joined in:

> We think it's really lovely. When you drive round the Island you are struck by the variety: these picturesque little bays on the north coast and then the big west coast St Ouen's Bay, very similar with its dunes to the Atlantic coast of France. And we've found it all so peaceful with friendly people, and it's so clean. We've been into St Helier a couple of times and, unlike home, you always seem to be able to find a parking space. [I told Jeremy that we locals were not always as generous in our comments.]

Ruth then told me about some of the family's other activities, including a visit to the War Tunnels ('quite interesting, since we didn't know much about the Occupation') and their experience of the Battle of Flowers.

> It said on the programme that the Carnival Procession started at 1.30 and the Main Procession at 2.30. But by a quarter to three we had only seen two things. There seemed to be terrible delays and, despite the floats being beautiful, there were far too many gaps and not much of a carnival atmosphere. Mind you, there was a massive storm beforehand and we got absolutely drenched as we stood there for an hour and a half waiting for things to happen. Towards the end the exhibits seemed to bunch up and it all got going a bit.

Beau Couperon Hotel

By this time, young son Ben had joined us. I learned that they had all been swimming at Plémont, with the children having some very good belly-boarding there, as well as jumping off the pier at Bonne Nuit on another day. I asked Ben what he thought of his Jersey holiday. He was sorry to be going home soon and, to my question about the best bits, his answer was unsurprising: 'The beaches.'

~

I wandered into the Beau Couperon Hotel and was given good help by the Polish girl on duty. I knew that many Kenyans now worked in Jersey's hospitality industry and I was anxious to chat with one of them. I was introduced to Hannah Macharia and she agreed to answer my questions. We sat below the seaward wall of the hotel which, incidentally, has a story of its own: it is what is left of Rozel Barracks, with this frontage on the beach very much still in its original state.

Hannah told me that she lived in Nairobi, having gone to school there and then attended college – a two-year course in housekeeping and laundry. The college was visited by officials of Jersey Tourism recruiting for the Island's hotels, and hence her reason for being here at Rozel.

> This was three years ago and I have worked each season at the Beau Couperon. For my first six months I was housekeeping, but I then moved to the restaurant as a waitress and I like it better – one is more in touch with the guests and with different people to talk to.
>
> I had heard of Jersey before, but it was the wrong one – the one in America. I had never been to Britain before. The Tourism people paid my fare, but I have repaid it with deductions from my wages. No, I don't swim in the sea. I had seen the sea a long time ago at Mombasa when I was very young, but Nairobi is a long way from the ocean. On my days off I go round the Island and visit friends. The hotel has a staff car and we can hire it for these trips. I am hoping to go home for a few months in January but shall probably come back for another season. As to, say, ten years' time, perhaps I shall wish to stay in Kenya and run my own business.

I then asked Hannah whether there were any drawbacks to her working in Jersey. Her reply was a disturbing one.

Some of the people here are very friendly but some are racist. I have come across so many racists. One time in Town I was walking along a street and a woman said so that I could hear, 'Why don't we get the blacks out of Jersey?' And at times in the restaurant you find that some guests don't want me to serve them. Some are very nice but others are not. It is really strange. How do I cope? Well, the hotel management here are very kind and supportive; I have good companions and the Polish are very friendly; I also have several Kenyan friends and we console each other. But I have to say, that is the down side.

~

With an abiding sense of shame I left Beau Couperon, crossed the road and took the steep path opposite, up through the grounds of Chateau La Chaire hotel. I wanted to find out more about Samuel Curtis's world-renowned Victorian garden and about the recent much publicised plans to restore it. The hotel receptionist gave me relevant details about Angie Petkovic and I rang her in Cheltenham and subsequently wrote to her with a number of questions. Angie has a career background in PR, marketing and customer services. She has long experience in tourism and the leisure sector and came to Jersey in January 2001 to meet her then new client, Chateau La Chaire.

It was on a misty wet morning that I took my first walk into the garden and became completely captivated by the topography and feel of the place. After research I found that here was a wonderful opportunity for restoration. This was something unique in the British Isles and in a wonderful destination. It had the potential to be one of the top ten garden attractions in Europe.

My partner and I invested much time and money in getting all the facts together for presentation to the States and in due course we received the promise of £1.3m for project commencement. We encountered many difficulties in trying to make progress and I have learned today [2.9.04] that our planning application has been turned down.

I was brought up never to regret, but I do have a regret: that this wonderful garden with all its charm, history and uniqueness is here in Jersey, and I have failed to get the people of Jersey to allow us to take forward its restoration. Perhaps if it had been a Jersey person starting it or taking it over, then the development might have been viewed more favourably. For myself, I just want to see the garden brought back to life, even though my involvement has now ended. Samuel Curtis's garden feeds the soul and mine is starved.

~

I left Chateau La Chaire and made my way down the Vallée de Rozel, passing the famous pink tulip and handkerchief trees which are spectacular in the spring (but less so in what was now high summer). Before resuming my journey east I popped into the Rozel Bay Hotel for a pint of Bass and a sandwich and then tackled the steep hill out of the village, arriving near the top at Le Frère (under previous ownership known as Bistro Frère) where I wanted to meet its head chef, Stephane Goujeau. I managed to haul Stephane out of the kitchen and he told me something of his early life and of his six or seven years in Jersey. He was born and brought up in Limoges and went to the school for chefs at Souillac where he learned all the traditional French cooking skills. After four years there he went and worked in Switzerland where he met and married his wife who is Portuguese and from Madeira. She had relations in Jersey and it was this that brought them to the Island in 1997.

My first job here was at the Royal Hotel in David Place but I have been at Le Frère for almost six years. You ask whether my style of cooking has changed since that early training in France. Here I have had the opportunity to work with English, Irish, Scots, Germans and Australians, and one is learning all the time, while still practising those basic principles of cooking. Good food, different flavours, excellent presentation, these are so important. And presentation must be perfect: the view of the dish and then the taste of it. It is such a rewarding job here, and Jersey produce is so good and varied: lots of fresh fish, oysters, rich dairy products, nice cream, strawberries, tomatoes and so much else.

I have a brigade of five in the kitchen here, and of course we work a split shift. But this for me is not inconvenient; it is the life I like and I get back in the afternoon for a little break and to see the family. The restaurant opened under new ownership in March and the redecoration has made it brighter and warmer. We have had a very good summer, doing lots of business.

As to living in Jersey, the language was a problem at first but my English is now better (though it is beginning to go downhill again, with several French chefs in the kitchen). I like the Island because it is small. Big cities are not for me. The only thing is the expense of living here and the accommodation difficulties when one does not have housing qualifications.

With the French coast ten miles away and very visible on this clear, sunny day through the restaurant windows, I asked Stephane whether he was ever homesick.

Not at all. Actually I have never been in that part of France even on a day trip, nor to Sark or Guernsey. I am very happy here in Jersey.

On that optimistic note we made our farewells and Stephane went back to the kitchen where the day's bread was being baked and preparations were being made for the busy lunchtime session.

~

Leaving Le Frère I now took the path to the left, La Rue des Fontonelles (the road of little fountains), which wound its way down to Saie Harbour and, just before it, the Dolmen du Couperon. The nineteenth century historians thought

that Jersey's many dolmens were Druidic temples but these days we know better. They are in fact prehistoric burial places, and this particular dolmen is a long cist, or *allée couverte*, excavated and restored in 1868.

Saie Harbour is the easternmost bay on the north coast and its cart-track, hewn out of the rock, was used for the removal of *vraic*, seaweed for feeding the soil. It is here that the

Dolmen du Couperon

La Coupe

round-the-island walker has a choice: either to head over the rocks and sand to La Coupe and the hillock in the distance with its little tower or to take the easier option of the tarmac up from the harbour and then down to one of Jersey's loneliest little coves. I did the latter and came along the road to the house 100 feet above the beach built in 1952 by Sylvia Biggar and her late husband Nigel. But before calling on her, I pushed my way through the undergrowth up to the headland point with its Napoleonic-era Royal Navy look-out post. Fortunately there seemed to be no enemy French ships approaching, and I returned to *Costa Brava* (for that is the house's name) and rang the front door bell.

Mrs Biggar led me into her sitting room with its staggering panoramic views of the Ecrehos and the French coast and told me something of her family background: a Jersey grandmother and a father born in the Island but working as an artist for much of his life in England. She trained as an architect and came to Jersey in 1947 to join her parents who had by then retired here. Fellow-architect Nigel gave her a job – at £5 a week ('I thought it was quite a lot of money in those days') – and in 1951 they married.

> We designed the house together. Originally the land around it was part of the Rozel Manor estate and we bought it for very little. We just thought the situation was lovely and we wanted to build a house here. We applied to the States and the Beauté Naturelle committee came out, stumped around and said that they didn't see why we shouldn't, so long as we were prepared to extend the little car park at the bottom. We agreed, cut some bushes down and that was that.
>
> Nigel died 11 years ago, and I have now lived here for over 50 years. Do I ever tire of the view? Never, never, because it's always changing – sunny in the morning and storm in the afternoon. I don't think that I could ever leave it. People say, 'Oh, aren't you

lonely out here?' Well, I am lonely on my own, but the dogs keep me lively, and it would probably kill me if I moved.

I then asked Mrs Biggar about her wonderful recent gift of the land at La Coupe to the National Trust for Jersey. She told me that she had never been an active member of the Trust but that she and Nigel had in the past vaguely discussed the matter. She was anxious to safeguard this exceptional part of the Island for the future, very much hoping that no enlarged car park would be a part of any future plans. 'That would be the end of La Coupe as it is.' My final question was whether she was herself a boat person. This was her reply:

> We started off with a little 20ft speedboat. Nigel didn't tell me anything about it. He took me down to the beach where he had brought round the new purchase. 'This is for you,' he said. We embarked and in rough seas went over to the end of the St Catherine's breakwater. I was so terrified that I refused to come back with him and walked all the way home instead. But after that I came round to the idea, and we did in due course have a succession of three fairly large cabin cruisers.

~

There is no path along the coast from La Coupe and I therefore made my way by the lanes, coming down the Rue de la Perruque to the little beach of Flicquet, with St Catherine's breakwater not far off to the south. For years I had always wondered about the history of the strange house here, possessing a touch of 'Gothic' as though it were out of a horror film and, misguidedly perhaps, called Flicquet Castle. I took courage and rang the bell which was answered by a friendly dog and a charming Irishman, Vincent Hickey. He invited me in and quickly put me in the picture.

> I am a plasterer by trade, specialising in decorative ceilings, mouldings and that kind of thing but, being an Irishman, I can of course do a bit of everything. Flicquet Castle is owned by Marshall Doran who came to Jersey in the 1950s and bought the Revere Hotel in Kensington Place. He also owns a hotel in County Mayo and spends much time there, and we got to know each other with me doing work for him. I come over here each year for six months or so and do repair jobs on this property.
> In 1956-7 Marshall came out to Flicquet where there were

two cottages, this being one of them. He loves castles, armour and old things, and he built this house from his head. This was his vision, his inspiration. That fireplace there comes from the house where Lillie Langtry was born. Forty years ago, old granite buildings were being knocked down and Marshall would buy up the stone, and the house has been steadily worked on from that time.

Marshall Doran has known me for getting on 30 years and this is my fourth year here. I came originally to do the roof, but all the floors have now been renewed and I am here to make sure that repairs get done. When I saw Flicquet for the first time I fell in love with the place. To me the house should look its best and that's why I stick with it.

I had previously only heard of Jersey from watching *Bergerac* on TV, but I love the people and the Island. At 48 I can just remember Ireland when nobody had anything. Now there's an awful lot of money and it's a much less friendly place than it was. To me Jersey is a lot like Ireland was years ago.

I'm not one for swimming but I like the seaweed. In my part of Ireland there are several seaweed baths – great for the treatment of arthritis and the skin. I've tried some of the Jersey seaweed in the bath here. It's slightly different though.

Flicquet Castle

~

I left the non-arthritic Vincent Hickey with his glowing skin. Out to sea I saw the replica of Captain Cook's *Endeavour* passing under full sail for St Helier. I took the path to St Catherine's – up the lane and then left through a little wood.

Until the 1840s this was a wild and inaccessible part of Jersey, and it was here in 1847 that the British government made the decision, as it turned out as misguided as the decision in the 1990s to construct the Millennium Dome, to build a deep-water harbour. Hundreds of workmen were imported; thousands of tons of granite were quarried (you can see the scars nearby); over £$\frac{1}{2}$ million were spent and a road built. In the middle of the programme the advent of steamships made the whole project obsolete. The plans for the other huge harbour arm from Archirondel were abandoned, and in due course the 'white elephant' northern breakwater was handed over to the States.

One person in particular could tell me more about all this: Mary Phillips, local historian and broadcaster. I arranged to have coffee with her at the Museum Brasserie in Town and, with my Dictaphone on the table, she told me first about her early life.

> I was born in Dolgellau, living in this Welsh community and speaking both Welsh and English. In due course I went to the University of Wales at Aberystwyth and had a wonderful time there reading English. After that I took up librarianship, first in the St Peter's Square Library in Manchester and then as assistant county librarian back in Merionethshire. After marriage to David who worked for Barclays Bank we came to Jersey in 1958. For years after my children were born I taught – first Music in various schools and then History at JCG. When BBC Radio Jersey started up in 1982 I began broadcasting, having met the station manager at a party and asking him whether he was short of programme ideas. So I started doing talks about walking round the Island and have been broadcasting about the Island's history ever since. I am still at it, writing something new every week and researching in the Société library or in the reference section of the library in Halkett Place.

In the late 1980s the BBC had published some of Mary's broadcast talks as *Tracks and Tales: 21 Coastal Walks*. I knew that she was working on a book about St Catherine's breakwater and I wanted to share some of what her researches had revealed. She first told me what had fired her interest in this particular subject.

I love St Catherine's as a place. Look at it from any angle and you see how the breakwater fits into the background. And the quarrying changed the landscape of the area; otherwise the cliffs would still come down sheer to the coast.

One of the remarkable facts was the speed with which the work progressed – the stone done by craftsmen-masons and the necessary wooden structures by skilled carpenters. And the construction used horses, taking the stone and rubble along railway lines, rather than machines.

Why was it built? The Duke of Wellington, that old warhorse, claimed to have discovered through his spies that the French were fortifying and strengthening their channel ports. So the British parliament was persuaded to sanction the construction of harbours of refuge to meet the supposed threat. And with steam ships coming in, there was a need for bigger ports with more space for manoeuvring. Alderney and Jersey were closest to France and these two projects went ahead. Here in Jersey there were disputes as to where the harbour should be, with Constables each rooting for their own parishes. Bouley Bay, Noirmont and St Catherine's were all candidates. The one man who was the authority on tides around the Island, Captain Martin White RN, was not consulted. He knew that at St Catherine's the breakwater would cause the currents to change and the prospective harbour to silt up. The right people were not approached and the French threat had been exaggerated. In today's money this botched St Catherine's project cost many millions.

Mary Phillips had some very interesting insights into the social history associated with the breakwater's construction.

Those working on its building were housed in various ways: places specially constructed for them; sleeping in the Martello towers or in barns; many living in Gorey and doing the trek there and back each day. Some brought families and wives, and at one time there were 500 or so around this small corner of the Island. L'Hôpital, still standing and with hooks inside for hammocks, was for the sick and injured (though few were killed in the construction and a cholera epidemic was successfully contained). There was a school for 60 children, used also for band rehearsals and meetings. There were two chapels and a pub – in other words a thriving community. After the whole thing came to an end, many of those involved stayed on with their wives and families or married local girls. It could be said that they melted into the landscape.

With the tape running out and the coffee cups empty, I asked Mary for her final thoughts on St Catherine's.

> Those who commissioned the work had been warned: they ignored Martin White and his knowledge of the tides. The right people weren't asked.
>
> But what were we left with? A great feat of engineering which enhances a wonderful corner of the Island. Those who are getting on a bit and can't walk very well can still tackle the half-mile out to sea and the half-mile back, away from traffic noise and breathing fresh air. It was all so skilfully done and I tramp along the breakwater, even when the weather is awful, marvelling at what was achieved – even though the result of all this labour, as far as it concerned defence of the realm, was so fruitless.

~

Before continuing my journey I took Mary Phillips's advice and felt obliged to do the walk to the end of the breakwater and back. Fishing over the north wall, with a couple of young sons and several rods, was Russell Minchington, a postman with a round in Grouville. He had just landed a fish as I approached but had thrown it back. We got talking.

> I suppose I come and fish here about 25-30 times a year. Different parts of the breakwater are best for different fish. I only use this spot for rock fish or, to give them their proper name, wrasse. I'm using crab for bait. If they're a decent size – over 4 lbs – I keep them and take them home for cooking. They taste lovely; fillet and then bake them for about 45 minutes.
>
> There's good night fishing for conger all around the breakwater. I might come from 6 pm and leave in the early hours of the morning. And it's very rare to leave without anything. Of course there are times when you can be here for eight hours and catch nothing, but that's not often.
>
> Fishing is my main hobby; very relaxing, getting me away. Today the weather's not favourable – the wind's too strong and there's a

neap tide. The bigger tides bring in more fish. I and my boys been here this afternoon for about four hours, and that fish you saw me catch has been my first today, and sadly it was too small to keep.

~

I reached the end of the breakwater and came back lower down on its south side. Passing the Morning Watch Tackle Shop, I popped in to have a word with Mark Symons, its proprietor. Mark is a Jerseyman who after school first went in to the butchery business and then in due course became a chef cooking pub grub. He has had this business for eight years. He showed me a photo, undoubtedly his pride and joy: Mark holding up a massive conger eel and the inscription at the base of the frame reading, 2003 CONGER SHORE CHAMPION – 40LB 12OZ.

They can get larger. This one I caught last year in the conger angling festival – off the breakwater, just outside the shop. I used cuttle fish as a bait. Fishing here, you have good and bad days. But there's a great range of species – bream, mackerel, dogfish, conger, ray, the odd sunfish and so on. This is a popular place for fishing of course. We get quite a lot of visitors too, not only locals. Yesterday we had 14 people from Wales and one of them caught a lobster – with a rod, catching the hook in the claws. And the rewards of it all? A bit of patience and the pleasure of eating the supper that you have caught yourself.

Breakwater, St. Catherine's

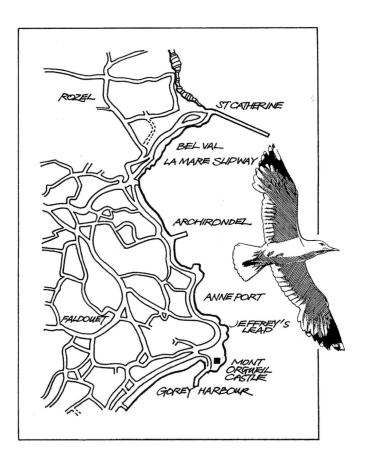

10

St Catherine's to Gorey Harbour

On completing my stroll out to sea and back, I headed south along the road, noting on the right the *viviers* where the German bunker and tunnels have been put to good use by the fish trade and on the left the St Catherine's sailing club, with part of its premises 150 years before having been the carpenters' workshop for the breakwater builders. At Bel Val I took the path which lies above the shore and below the road and, just before the La Mare slipway, passed below the now boarded-up house, L'Hôpital, which Mary Phillips had mentioned. Here too is the St Catherine's lifeboat station, and a notice on its walls announced that Bruce Ferguson (with telephone number) was the senior helmsman. In due course I contacted him and arranged to give him a bite of lunch at the Bistrot Central. At the appointed time I awaited the arrival of, perhaps, a sturdy bearded sea-dog. Instead, in came a dapper, besuited trust fund manager who had been educated at Victoria College. Bruce told me that he had spent much of his youth dinghy sailing at St Catherine's and that he had at first considered the Royal Navy as a career, having passed the selection procedures for Dartmouth, but decided instead to work in the Island's finance industry.

> It all began in 1987 when, on a trip to the Ecrehos, I got chatting to Roy Bullen, local secretary of the RNLI, and we saw the St Catherine's lifeboat on an exercise. The following week I received a phone call from the then senior helmsman: 'I hear you want to join the lifeboat.' It was the press gang in action.

Lifeboat station, La Mare slipway

I've been senior helmsman since 1996. The official retirement age is 45 and I understand why: when you have been out to sea for three or four hours you take quite a pounding, with the odd bump or bruise. We have 15 sea-going members, broken up into three crews, with each crew on duty one week in three. We get on average about 25 call-outs a year, and these tend to be in the summer months. Our inshore boat is capable of operating 45 miles from station on full fuel tanks, but our usual operations are covering the south-east corner of the Island, the east coast and towards France. Carteret has tidal locks, and we are sometimes called out to deal with things over there when for this reason their lifeboat cannot get out of harbour.

You ask what has been my hairiest experience. Fortunately there have not been too many. But the one that stands out was four or five years ago just before Christmas. We were called out at 4 a.m.; there had been a report that a six-metre inflatable had broken down off Jersey's north coast. The wind was force 6/7 and we went out looking for them. We began sweep-searching the area as the weather deteriorated. It was blowing 7/gusting 9 and we found ourselves off the French coast in big seas with waves five metres high and very steep. By this point we had handed the search over to larger vessels and we started to head back for the Island. On two occasions the boat nearly capsized, standing on its stern with the engines fully submerged, dropping off the top of a wave and falling into the trough on the other side. At one point I looked back and the crew behind me were submerged below the water. We lost our main radio and our satellite navigation. Two days before I had watched a programme about the Penlee lifeboat disaster which had also been around Christmas time. And in my mind was the thought of getting back to shore safely with my crew. We stopped at the Ecrehos for a breather and it took another hour punching through the seas back to St Catherine's. When I got off the boat I went and sat in a corner – quite emotional for a time and glad that we were back on *terra firma*. And what was particularly galling was the fact that the individuals for whom we had gone out to search were washed up on the French coast and were almost certainly up to no good – or they would not have been out in those conditions at that time of year. Our own lives had been risked by others who were probably engaged in criminal activity.

My wife and family are very tolerant and put up with the worry and an element of family disruption. When I'm on duty I have to remain sober, ready to drop everything and run if the pager goes off. And my motivation? The satisfaction and enjoyment that I used to get from sailing. And I would like to think that, if I were out there and needed help, someone would be willing to come to my rescue.

~

Archirondel Tower

Archirondel, with its popular Driftwood Café, was now only a short step round the rim of the bay. A sign told me more about its prominent tower:

> **Archirondel Tower – La Roche Rondel**
> **1793-4 – prototype (with gun platforms)**
> **for La Rocco Tower, St Ouen,**
> **begun in 1796**

Incidentally the wall connecting the tower to the land is the first and only part constructed of what was to be the second St Catherine's breakwater.

I had with me, in French actually, a leaflet produced by Jersey Tourism entitled *Promenades à Jersey*, and the guide to many of the walks listed in it is Sue Hardy who on occasions during the summer months leads a St Martin Meander which includes Archirondel and this stretch of coast. I sought her out at her home in St Lawrence in order to find out more about her considerable knowledge of the Island and her work for the tourist industry.

Sue was anxious to tell me that the St Martin walk was far from her home stamping ground. Her mother was a Vibert from St Ouen and I quickly sensed that this was where her strongest affections lay: a family childhood in this western parish, with no cars, Shanks's pony, bicycles, donkeys, goats, horses and picnics on the sand dunes and at the dolmen.

I became fascinated with the Island from an early age, with my mother feeding us knowledge of its folklore and superstitions. I joined the Société in the '60s and became an active member of the National Trust some years later, first as a volunteer at Quetivel Mill and then as a member of its Council.

In the early 1990s Mike Stentiford and I got together with others, and out of this emerged the Jersey Walking Group. Our first event was in St Lawrence – my patch. We decided to meet at Morel Farm and 650 turned up. Our third walk was at St Catherine's. It was a bad day and yet there were 100 takers. All this acted as the forerunner for the book which appeared in 1992 of Island walks, edited by Beth Lloyd, with Mike Stentiford doing the nature notes and myself planning the routes and providing the information.

It was in the mid-1990s that Tourism introduced the Blue Badge guide scheme. It's a national organisation that monitors guiding standards. I became very involved in getting the walks on a proper footing and ended up as chairman of the local tour guides' association, producing its monthly newsletter for a time.

The numbers coming on the walks vary, of course. There may be a day with abysmal weather and no one show up at all, but there are particularly good attendances for the urban and suburban locations. Gorey is always popular as are St Helier and St Aubin. The Town tours are the staple diet.

My own favourite walk has to be round my own stamping-ground of St Ouen, taking people over the National Trust land where we picnicked as children, across to the dolmen and revealing that magnificent panorama of St Ouen's Pond, Rocco Tower and Corbière lighthouse. Is there a more wonderful sight?

I went on to ask Sue for her thoughts on the future of Jersey's tourist industry, and she told me of her optimism so long as air fares were reasonable, with the Island not being over-developed and its beauty preserved – the cliffs, the bays, the country lanes. She also sees the potential for developing the appeal of Jersey's great heritage, with people excited by its many layers of history. Was she, I asked, still taking up the cudgels for these causes?

I was once full of fervour at protesting. I think of the neglect of the stone walls and the contempt of motorists in driving up roadside banks and that sort of thing. It is very distressing. But as far as campaigning goes I have relaxed a little; one gets punch-drunk. I have sometimes felt like the little boy with his finger in the dyke. There is the horror of those Albert Pier flats masking Maritime House and the shadows they cast in the evenings on the visiting yachts in the marina. And then there are the concrete cobs west of Albert piling up a pong for the future with rotting seaweed and rats. I walk people around the old harbours and show them these incredible works of beauty, strength and ingenuity. What a contrast!

But, despite what is wrong, Jersey has that pull. When you come back, you look out of the aircraft window and see below you this little island in the sea. There is something more than just the beauty and the need to safeguard it as a green and pleasant place. There is its special culture, its unique history, and this gives one hope. There is comfort, when despairing at the faults of some modern developments, in considering our forebears in the early 18th century, say, putting up an archway and carving their initials on it. Look at them! But now we see it as part of our heritage. In other words, I cannot change the world; the world will change, and I must accept that.

~

Mont Orgueil and Gorey Harbour were now not far away. There was no longer a coast path and the road became my way ahead. I soon passed the new Moonraker apartments, impressive Art Deco pastiche and, I thought, sitting well in this environment, and more flats and houses going up on the site of the demolished Les Arches hotel. Hopefully that will be that, and this coast will not descend into a Costa Brava ribbon development.

A help to me throughout my Island journey has been the popular book, *Jersey Rambles*. Its author is John Le Dain and this is the pen name of Roger Jones, whose Seaflower Books has published many titles with Jersey subject-matter (this book is one, and another is my *Speaking of Jersey* which came out in 2003). As I approached Anne Port, with the road just above the shingle beach, I recalled that Roger had spoken well of it in his walking guide: 'This small bay, without so much as a beach café or a deck chair, is a personal favourite. At mid and low tide a fine sandy beach is exposed and the gentle shelving here makes for good swimming'.

I was not prepared for a dip but I thought it would be good to seek out Roger and find out more about him. He was born of a Jersey mother in 1945 and brought up in Chiswick. In due course he went to the University of York and took a degree in Social Science. After working as a gardener for a local authority he accepted a job at Chiswick Public Library and did a post-graduate course in librarianship. In 1980 he moved to Bradford on Avon, took over a bookshop and gradually built up his bookselling in tandem with his publishing business.

> I decided to branch out into publishing books on the Channel Islands, the first of which was my *Jersey Rambles* in 1992, having already published various English walking guides. *Jersey Rambles* consistently sells a 1000 copies a year, and we will be shortly publishing our twenty-seventh Seaflower title.
>
> This part of the east coast, just north of Gorey and with France not far off, is a great favourite of mine, with its quiet, natural, countryside-meets-the sea character. And Anne Port's special virtue is that it is not commercialised and you can swim there at any state of the tide.
>
> What to me is the special quality of Jersey? It has been my second home throughout my life, my one constant. I love the beaches, the meeting-point of land and sea, the feel of sand between the toes, the pleasures of swimming. And there's Jersey's granite, its other rocks, its flora and fauna and its extraordinarily rich variety of landscapes. I am passionate about the Island's sheer physical beauty.
>
> My wife Hazel and I are about to make Jersey our permanent home, living here throughout the year as opposed to holidays. Seaflower Books will continue to publish, and my Jersey family history beckons me to indulge in further investigation of it.

~

Up the road from Anne Port I passed the sad, boarded up 'Tudorbethan' house which used years ago to serve cream teas. Just past it, a National Trust for Jersey granite stone announced our location: Le Saut Geffroy. The story of Geoffrey's Leap is well known: a criminal called Geoffrey was guilty of a crime, the punishment for which was death. Over this high rock he went and surprisingly survived, witnessed by a big crowd as he swam to the shore. Opinion was divided as to what should now be done: free him or throw him over again. Geoffrey decided to show off, throw himself over and demonstrate to the crowd how easy it was to survive. This time he miscalculated: a poor leap, a dashed head on the rocks below and death by drowning.

Not dwelling too long on this preposterous story, I came round the corner of the road with, before me, what must surely be Jersey's greatest and most famous historical monument, Gorey Castle, named Mont Orgueil – Mount Pride – by Henry V's brother, the Duke of Clarence. It was started between 1180 and 1212 on the orders of King John, has been besieged at various times by the French, was in the 16th century, not being impervious to cannon, superseded in the Island's defences by the construction of Elizabeth Castle in St Aubin's Bay but saved from subsequent demolition on the orders of Sir Walter Raleigh when Governor who gave his opinion on the matter: 'It is a stately fort of great capacity. It were a pity to cast it down.' So there it is today, having been during the Occupation 60 years and more ago a large German headquarters with a machine gun post constructed on the top (which is still there and very visible). In recent years the Castle and its renovation have been the cause of much controversy and dispute. It was time for me to find out more about these fierce squabbles, and my first port of call was the home, above Gorey Harbour, of Jurat John de Veulle, Chairman of Jersey Heritage Trust which has responsibility in this matter.

John, of Jersey parents, was actually born in Ealing and educated at Haileybury and then at Trinity College, Dublin, where he read Economics and Politics. He had spent all his school and university holidays in the Island and came home permanently in 1967 as a young chartered accountant. Years later he was the Jersey senior partner of Ernst and Young, 'cock at the top of the dung heap' as he graphically put it, and took retirement – of a sort – in 1994. He was elected one of the Island's 12 Jurats in 1995 and I first asked him about this.

I have found it a means of contributing to Jersey, having spent a very busy professional life and not having previously been involved in the honorary system. Politics did not attract me; my father had been Deputy for St Clement and had become very disillusioned with the inability of the States to make decisions and get things done. So as a Jurat I could quietly roll up my sleeves, not realising at first how much work was to be involved as the Royal Court load, over the last decade, has become so much greater. I was proud to be elected one of the two Lieutenant-Bailiffs in 1999 which means that I sometimes preside over the Court and am to some extent one of the leaders of the Jurats' team.

I now wanted to get on to the Heritage Trust and the Mont Orgueil controversies and guided the conversation in that direction, discovering that the Heritage Trust had been founded in 1984 by the States as a means to channel States money into the work of the Société Jersiaise and heritage generally. John had been involved with the Trust's work for some years before taking over as Chairman in 2000. He was at once landed with two fairly hot potatoes: the drying-up of revenue from declining visitor numbers with the States unwilling to make up the deficit, and the questions arising over the restoration and repair of Mont Orgueil.

Our main objective with the Castle was to repair and restore, dealing with urgent matters and stopping further deterioration. The roof of the medieval hall was in a state of semi-collapse, and we completed this necessary task. The other important wind-and-watertight job was the whole of the south part of the castle – the residential apartments - and this too has been completed. The third big element was the so-called Tudor Great Hall which we wanted to roof over, not only for conservation but also since it is a puzzling place for visitors. There is no doubting that it was once roofed and floored, and we are replacing what was originally there. The history of it is all very woolly.

I had become chairman in June 2000 and the controversy over the 'Tudor' hall blew up in the autumn. FOMO – Friends of Mont Orgueil – was formed. I had no difficulty with open and reasonable discussion on all these issues, but FOMO would write to the press and to third parties without getting in touch with us so that we could explain what we were doing and why. There was lack of communication and barriers were sadly thrown up fairly quickly.

FOMO did not want the 'Tudor' hall roofed; that was their fundamental objection; they considered that it should be left open for people to admire a noble ruin. But leaving it was not an option, and the satisfactory way forward was to recapture the area, approaching the way it was built in the first place. There were of course no drawings or plans originally, and there had to be an element of deduction. A problematic area was the east wall of the 'Tudor' hall, a chunk of wall totally missing and no one knowing what was there.

Eventually the whole difficult business was resolved by the States planners calling in an independent expert. The outcome was permission being granted for 140 or our 150 submissions.

The 'Tudor' hall plans go ahead but we failed to get sanction for the proposed outside staircase which had been taken down in 1911. It was for us a relatively happy outcome and we have, importantly, gained a set process for future applications of this sort which will apply for any similar bids for sites such as St Aubin's Fort or Elizabeth Castle. We now have a set planning procedure for ancient monuments and this is a vital outcome for the Island.

And my main worries concerning Jersey's heritage? I am most anxious about the understanding of these issues by the 52 members of the States. They talk about 'heritage' but know little about it. I listened to two debates concerning Mont Orgueil and I was astonished and amazed. If that is the care and attention which they bring to the question of income tax or social security, then Heaven help us.

A final thought is this: we are establishing greater co-ordination between the Heritage Trust and the Société Jersiaise and, hopefully in due course, the National Trust for Jersey; and there is the hope of better co-operation in the future in the whole area of heritage sites.

Mont Orgueil

Having heard the official line concerning Mont Orgueil, it was now time to take in another point of view. I sought out John Mesch, tough FOMO member and doughty fighter and defender of the eastern coastline, at his home just above Archirondel. John was born in Jersey and claims that as a young child in 1940 he was on the third last boat to England before the Island was occupied by the Germans. He and family came back to Jersey in September 1945. He went to school at Victoria College and then decided on a service career – Sandhurst and a commission in the Royal Artillery. He retired from the Army in 1988 and came to live in a part of the Island familiar from his boyhood days – cycling out to Bel Val and fishing off the breakwater at St Catherine's.

He has been active over the years in campaigning to preserve sensitive sites between St Catherine's and Gorey, the first threat, successfully challenged, being the proposed development of a restaurant at the St Catherine's *vivier*. Since then there have been controversies over Moonraker, the Springtide site at Archirondel, the Les Arches development and two concerns at Anne Port – the hotel and the fishermen's cottages. Unsurprisingly he has firm views on the politicians, planners and planning.

> This is my philosophy: the politicians have but one function which is to make good policy satisfying the aspirations of the people. The policy, having been established, should be brought under the law. The politicians should not go against that policy. If it is to be reformed, then the law should be adjusted accordingly. And at present we have an odd situation: the new Island Plan has been fully drafted and endorsed by the States in 2002. But it is still not formally under the law. When I write letters to States committees it is to draw their attention to what the actual policy is. Why should I have to do this? If the policy is good, they should abide by it. If it is not good, they should remake the policy. As to this eastern coast, I have seen how the St Clement coastline has been destroyed in my lifetime, with filling in and over-development. Is the outstanding character of this part of the Island going to go the same way?

I now invited John Mesch to consider Mont Orgueil and its controversies. He did not mince his words.

> I believe the crux of the matter was this: the Jersey Heritage Trust decided that the castle should be the flagship for the 800th celebrations of 2004, and a major part of their plan was to

reconstruct this Tudor Great Hall which in fact is neither a hall nor Tudor. They went to the tourist investment fund and got £3m for the development. I wrote and told them that they needed a conservation plan; on completion it emerged as fiction and they stuck to it. The whole basis was wrong. My military training told me that if you get the aim wrong, the outcome will be wrong. Their aim was to Disneyfy the castle for the visitor experience. They should have been saying that this is a major piece of Jersey's heritage, and their aim should have been to conserve and interpret the castle in the best possible way, accurately and historically. English Heritage is against speculative construction. No one can tell you when this 'hall' was roofed, what it was used for or what it looked like. You don't need a roof to preserve the castle.

My final thoughts? This unelected quango made an ill-considered plan, badly project-managed and involving the expenditure of large amounts of public money. Apparently we are going to get an 18 foot high statue of an allegorical wounded man, and then there's going to be a knight on a horse. We are also getting three new gardens – a waste of money. What right have these people to foist on us the Disneyfication of this great historic building?

~

I thought it expedient to remain neutral concerning these difficult and heat-generating matters. I left John Mesch, made my way to Gorey Harbour, tranquil at the foot of the Castle's impressive bulk, and gained some sustenance, sitting outside at The Dolphin, in the form of a crab sandwich and a pint of beer. I then walked along towards the pier, popping in to what has traditionally been know as the Harbourmaster's House which is home to the Gorey Interpretation Centre. This modern panelled display of information – with some particularly evocative old photographs – told me all I needed to know of Gorey Harbour: the 19th century oyster industry employing by the mid-1830s at least 2000 men and 100 or more women and girls; the church, the houses and cottages, all dating from this period; the ship-building industry, active until the 1890s when the coming of steam-powered, iron-build vessels put an end to it; and the railway which until the coming of the motor bus was for many years the main means of transport in to Town.

As I reached the pier-head the fast-ferry catamaran, *Victor Hugo*, came in from Carteret. After he had supervised its arrival, Adam Tranter, port operations officer, was able to spare me a few minutes and tell me about his job.

> I was born in Derby and moved here in 1970 at the age of nine when my father was appointed head of Les Quennevais School. I started working at the harbours in 1985, first as a marina attendant and labourer/driver. I was a diver for ten years and ended up as chief marine supervisor in charge of staff at three marinas before being promoted to this post in 2003.
>
> Gorey Harbour used to be fully manned until 2002. But these ferries, the only passenger shipping now, only come in here five times a month during the summer, and this does not warrant a full-time presence.

Adam evidently relishes his duties, primarily of course at the harbour in St Helier, and is dedicated to his life in Jersey.

> I have a lovely home at Petit Port in St Brelade and I do a little volunteer thing there: keeping an eye on the old Jersey Radio station at Corbière, the former German observation tower. Now I think you visited it early on in your Island journey [see chapter 4]. Well, it's now closed and the radio men now operate from Maritime House. But last Saturday was the National Trust Heritage Day and we had 500 visitors climbing to the top to see the control room and enjoy the view.

~

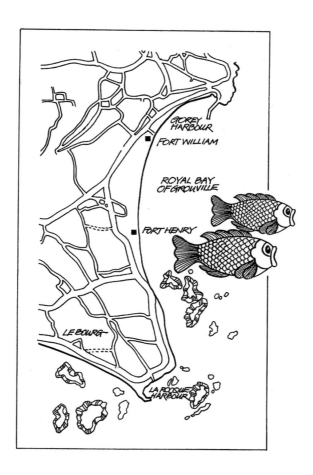

11

Gorey Harbour to La Rocque

As I stepped out towards what is described on the ordnance survey map as La Commune de Gouray, I was quickly reminded of my history lesson back at the Harbourmaster's House. Here by the pavement was a modern sculpture entitled **RECOLLECTION** and bearing this inscription:

**THIS SYMBOLIC KEEL
RECALLS THE NINETEENTH CENTURY
SHIPYARDS OF GOREY**

I was soon striding along the sea wall with the Common, much of its 71 acres leased by the Royal Jersey Golf Club, on my right. It was reputedly once a favoured venue for duelling, and for 60 years from 1843 it was the location for the Island's horse-racing (see the Ouless painting in the Museum art gallery and reproduced on the cover of Grouville's millennium volume, *The History of a Country Parish*). It soon became clear to me that one of the most striking features of the three or so miles from Gorey to La Rocque is the multitude of fortifications, most of them dating from the late 18th century, built on this stretch of coast which was particularly threatened by its proximity to France. Here at the northern end of the golf course are the outer walls of Fort William, built around 1760 and with its actual building incongruously replaced by a relatively modern house. Half a mile further on is Fort Henry, considered by some to be the single most important complex of Jersey's fortifications. I had spent the previous 15 minutes keeping a wary eye on the golfers as I walked along, passing notices suggesting firmly that I avoided any golf balls coming in my direction. It was time to find out more about the

Fort Henry

course, the club, its members and the game (my attitude to golf is of the 'good walk ruined' variety). I made a short diversion from the coast, crossed Le Grande Route des Sablons and rang Tony Turpin's front door bell.

Tony was born in 1911, became a junior member of the Royal Jersey in 1925 and re-joined after a break of some years in 1943. 'I have been a member for 66 years. It could have been 80. But despite that I am by far the longest serving member.' This was a morning when he was not on the links and was thus able to talk to me.

> My father was a schoolmaster. He was headmaster of St Mary's School and later of the technical school in La Motte Street. I went to St Mary's before going on to Victoria College and then to teacher training at St Luke's, Exeter. Having qualified I obtained a post at Grouville School (in what is now the parish hall). The children were delightful; they were children, not today's sophisticated semi-adults corrupted by the television.
>
> We moved into our new buildings a month after the outbreak of war. During the Occupation, with teacher shortage, I would start the year with a class of over 40. By 1945 I was given the title of deputy head; in 1951 I was appointed headmaster. I retired in 1971, having spent my whole career at the one school.

I wanted Tony to tell me about his golf and he recounted his first experiences hacking balls round on Ouaisné Common where the family had a holiday bungalow. Then came his schoolboy years as a member of the Royal Jersey until he went away to college and met his tennis-playing wife. During the Occupation tennis ceased, with the balls having lost their nap and being irreplaceable at the time, and he took up golf again. From 1945 to 1947 he was the club's honorary secretary until he made the case for a full-time paid successor, was for some years on the committee and, as head of the greens committee, was in charge of the course. Tony then told me how it had all started.

> William Laidlaw Purves, born in Edinburgh, promoted courses in the south of England. He knew that in Jersey there was a common on which a golf course could be laid out and sent a proxy over here, Francis Brewster. Brewster knew the ropes, joined the Victoria Club in Beresford Street, got together a group of people, surmounted various difficulties with the Constable of the parish and in March 1878 came out with a wheel-barrow, a hole-cutter and some metal spikes and laid out the course in a

day. And an interesting thing is this: if the railway had not been here, then there would have been no golf course and no members. They were the retired army and naval men and former civil servants living in the northern end of Town – Stopford Road, Midvale Road, Rouge Bouillon and so on. They were the backbone of the club, and to get to Grouville they had to catch the train, and the railway started in 1871. If there had been no train, there would have been no club.

Playing regularly and well into his tenth decade, Tony seemed relaxed about the changes over the years in the nature of the club and the game, telling me that from the start La Moye Golf Club would take businessmen while the Royal Jersey had been more exclusive (with concomitant financial problems), turning down those who were not deemed sufficiently gentlemanly. And lady members?

I don't object to the women on the course. Some men do resent them. I encounter quite a lot of them when I am playing and pass them a cheery greeting.

~

My curiosity about golf in general and the Royal Jersey in particular was not fully satisfied. To find out more I contacted Tommy Horton, for years the Club's pro, and visited him, just returned from a Seniors' tournament in Portugal, in his St Martin home. He told me of his Jersey forebears and that he should have been born in the Island had it not been for the Occupation and his mother's evacuation to St Helens in Lancashire. But he came to Jersey in 1945 and attended Grouville and then Hautlieu schools. I asked him how he started playing golf.

By the time I was five I had stolen one of my uncle's golf clubs and began hitting balls around. The family lived only 50 yards from the Royal Jersey, and I used to find golf balls on the course and want to hit them myself. Interestingly Harry Vardon, who first won the British Open in 1896, was born in Grouville on the edge of the golf course and just 250 yards from where I grew up. He and his friends when boys created their own little golf course on the right of the present twelfth hole, and this is exactly what my friends and I did 80 or so years later. We used to put baked bean tins in the ground and used a bamboo stick with a bit of cloth on it for a flag.

In due course I became a member of the artisans' section of the club and won various junior competitions. At the age of 15 there was a vacancy for the position of assistant pro. I went to see my headmaster. He said, 'Horton, you are never going to be a great scholar, but our secretary, Colonel Fry, tells me that you are a bloody good golfer, so I think you had better go and play golf.' So I did, and that was 1957.

After two years Tommy then took up golfing posts in England, being a regular on the European Tour in the 1960s, 1970s and 1980s and playing in two Ryder Cup matches – in 1975 and 1977. He came back to Jersey in 1975 to become pro at the Royal Jersey and stayed on until retirement in 1999 by which time he was achieving great success on the Seniors' Tour, winning 23 times, serving on the European Tour board of directors and chairing the Seniors' Tour committee. I now asked him what were the characteristics of the Royal Jersey course.

The Royal Jersey is mainly known because of Harry Vardon. It is now nearly 130 years old. It is a traditional links course, the term 'links' referring to the link land between the sea and the nearest agricultural land. It is only 95 acres and because of that would not be termed a championship course. In the old days it was a sandy waste and the golfers were highly skilled, with the ball lodging in little holes and footprints. Nowadays the fairways are almost perfect (but are never going to be quite like the inland swards you see on the TV), and the equipment now is so much better, with golf club heads being much larger and more forgiving. But the Royal Jersey will always be challenging, as are all links courses, with the sea breezes, the changeable weather and the tides affecting the wind direction perhaps two or three times in a round. And it's a narrow golf course, calling for some accuracy.

Before I left him I asked Tommy Horton whether he was a pessimist or optimist about the island where he grew up and which has been his home since returning in 1975. There was no doubting his response.

Sometimes I listen to the morning phone-in programme on Radio Jersey. It disappoints me to think that so many of those ringing in seem to consider that the Island is deteriorating. I am tempted to phone in myself one day and say, 'Please do an auction or something and buy these people a holiday somewhere else.' Let them go and find out what it is like in these other countries. They should be thankful that they live in such a marvellous place. Jersey's fantastic for bringing up children. We don't have Britain's inner city problems. Many people don't realise how lucky we are.

~

Before I resumed my walk there was one other person to see who lived close by, Rowland 'Chick' Anthony who for some years had served with me on the National Trust for Jersey's development applications committee. He has been known by all as Chick since, at the age of two and ready to go out, he was spotted all dressed in yellow by his grandmother who exclaimed, 'Oh, what a lovely little chick,' and that is how it has been ever since. His father was headmaster of St Martin's school and Chick, after schooldays at Victoria College, worked for the Meteorological Office and then, for many years, at the BBC as a sound engineer. He retired in 1989 and a few years later came back to the Island, inaugurating the environment section of the Société Jersiaise and taking on the editorship of Grouville's millennium book, *The History of a Country Parish*. He first told me about his special love for this stretch of coast.

> It is the expanse. We often walk down to the front across the golf course and sit there. There are not many specific features in it, but it has a special atmosphere of scale and scope. I often think that a child brought up with knowledge of this spectacle must have a very different outlook on life.

We chatted about the Mont Orgueil controversy (he tends to the FOMO point of view and considers that the Heritage Trust approach was wrong) and, perhaps surprisingly, considers that environmentally Jersey has not greatly changed since his boyhood.

> There are the built-up areas, but the colossal heart of the Island and the coastline are exactly as they were when I was a child. There are nasty bits – the monstrosity of the tower blocks and much of the new stuff in Town. But the architects' award competition is recognising buildings of quality; and yet it's a pity

that there are no wooden spoon awards as well. The new Island Plan is along the right lines, but I have to say that the waterfront development is so ugly and wrong on most counts.

Chick is a pro-Clothier man, doesn't want the Constables in the States unless elected in their own right and favours larger constituencies for States elections. He is also a great believer in the parish system.

> In England I eventually got into local politics – middle of the road and Liberal. I don't see that party politics need necessarily develop over here. Party politics does a lot of damage and it stifles independence which is still a characteristic of Jersey people. They are individuals who come together when required. Here in Grouville there is a very strong parish community feeling. I see the parish system as an important element of our Island life, and it is not necessarily under threat from new political arrangements.

~

It was time to move on, along the concrete promenade which separates the sea from the great variety of homes along this stretch of coast – pre-war Modernist examples, one or two striking recent buildings, some indifferent and neglected properties and even a Martello tower which one guide-book describes as having 'sprouted wings in its eagerness to be a house'. At La Rocque there is a Methodist chapel and, just before it, a charming cottage above the sea, the home of Jefferson Randles, Head of Art at Victoria College and the illustrator of this book. I called in to see him and, over a glass of wine and an expertly made Greek salad, he told me something of his early life.

> I was born and brought up in Doncaster and I did my degree in Fine Art, specialising in painting and drawing, at Hull. You see, I have always been drawn to places where there are big expanses of water. It's one of the fascinations of Jersey – with humankind having built harbours and piers, attempting to control these elemental forces, with that measure of nature always trying to overcome and break the structures down.
> Victoria College was my first teaching job. I started in January 1995 as the assistant to Robert Tilling. Robert was a great mentor, with his expectations for the students really high. He is a man passionate about the value of art, the philosophical as well as the

practical side, and the way in which art can be life-enriching. It was a privilege to work under him and a privilege to succeed him when he retired in 1997.

You ask me what is the particular reward for an artist living here by the sea. Hopefully I am inspired by many different landscapes, even a wasteland or an urban scene. But here on the coast one is more aware of the seasonal changes and the tides and their effect on the weather and the light. On a busy day the humdrum of life can be all-encompassing, but five or ten minutes out here gets things into perspective. The beauty of the Island and its landscape is a constant, enriching experience.

The task of illustrating *Journey Round Jersey* has given me, the art teacher, the motivation to get down to my own work. I have my targets and my deadlines; there is an element of excitement as this sense of self-discipline comes back. It's easy to be superficially familiar with a particular place, but to go back there and sit for an hour or two drawing opens up the intrinsic beauty, the feel, the spirit, the sense of place. That is what I am attempting to develop.

~

As I reached the slipway near the Seymour Inn, I looked out to the tower from which it derives its name. Seymour Tower, a mile or more out from the shore, sits on an islet called L'Avarison. It was built in 1782 and its square shape is unique among Jersey's coastal towers. Setting out at this low tide for a walk towards it was a party of 20 or so, being led on one of his well-known moonwalks by Andrew Syvret. Andrew, with a degree in Fisheries Science and having for several years been Coastal Officer for the States Planning and Environment Department, was the one to tell me more about this remarkable rockscape stretching before me. He first told me about his programme of guided walks.

I regularly do Rocco Tower in St Ouen's and Corbière lighthouse. Icho and Seymour are favourites, and the two towers on one tide are sometimes possible. And I have a new walk – from the pool at Havre des Pas, doing the entire bottom right-hand corner of the Island all the way up to Gorey, starting at high water and following the tide all the way round close to its perimeter. I was featured in the travel magazine of *The Independent* last August;

they nominated my night-time moonwalk to Seymour Tower their Walk of the Month.

Seymour Tower from La Rocque Harbour

I now asked Andrew what was special about this south-east coast?

Rocky shores, like this lunar landscape, are very rare. With others in this Norman-Breton gulf it is a fundamental engine-room of the English Channel, a very important diversity of habitat - lagoons and boulder fields where small things can grow unhindered and protected. This is one of the reasons why this coast was declared a Ramsar site – because it plays a vital role in the early life stages of a lot of the things that we like to eat when they grow up. It is a nursery, an incubator for lots of small animals and fish, lobsters, crabs, scallops and so on. Take the sea bass: the Jersey habitat, the shallow lagoons of La Rocque, these are their two- to five-year old habitats when they are putting on weight. They find a little sanctuary here.

What am I showing my visitors? Essentially we do three- or six-mile treks across the seabed and I talk about the animals, the birds and the seaweed that we find along the way. My most popular walk is the one to Seymour Tower, built, I point out, in 1782, a year after the Battle of Jersey. That's the way we do things here.

Andrew is making a very successful contribution to Jersey's tourist industry and has strong views about it.

> I am a *crapaud*, a genuine Jersey person, and I am very cynical about attempts to market the Island purely for fiscal reasons. I think that our preservation of the vernacular should come ahead of our marketing. The discerning tourist can see through the veneer. If I had a mission statement it would be, 'Let the habitat do the talking'. Don't Disneyfy our local culture and trivialise it. In other words, sell the unique identity of Jersey. If you contrive to sell them a chocolate box/Disney version, they will see straight through it.
>
> Perhaps the most astonishing thing about the south-east coast is the fact that the man who went on to be on the board of Jersey Zoo was the man who proposed in the States putting an international airport out there. While he was aware of the need to save species in Mauritius or Madagascar, he had no idea that on his own south-east coast was a habitat as worth preserving as anything the Zoo was trying to do in other parts of the world. It's that other half of Jersey, revealed when the tide is out, and it is this that keeps me sane.

~

I was now approaching La Rocque Harbour but, before walking out on its jetty, I noticed on the right, and lying back from the road, Seymour House, the handsome home of the Island's Attorney General, William Bailhache QC. He kindly agreed to have a chat with me and I called on him in the Law Officers' department at Mourier House opposite St Helier's Royal Square. Seymour House, built probably in the 1830s, has been his family home since 1984, and he spent his childhood further along the road at Le Hocq.

> We had a small boat when I was growing up – 12 feet long and called the Nancy Lee after my mother whose name was Nanette and my father Lee. All six of us used to go out in this boat, laden to the gunwales, when I was a kid. It was undoubtedly dangerous, and these days I suppose I would have to consider prosecuting my father for using it!

Schooldays at Charterhouse and then university years at Merton College,

Oxford, followed before reading for the Bar. When his elder brother Philip became Solicitor General in 1975, William came back to take his place in the family law firm and was in private practice until his appointment as Attorney General in the year 2000. Curious to know precisely the role of the Attorney General, I was directed to the States of Jersey website which told me all: 'The Attorney General and the Solicitor General are the Law Officers of the Crown and, among other functions, are the legal advisers of the States...They are members of the States' Assembly by virtue of their respective offices...They have the right to speak on all matters of States business but not to vote...By convention, they do not generally speak on political matters, other than those in which they have a direct official interest...'

I quizzed the Attorney General more closely about his, to some, controversial presence in the States.

> There are two reasons why it is important for the Attorney General to have an unfettered voice in the States. The first is that there are some quite difficult constitutional, legal or structural issues that come up from time to time for debate, and I think that the States gets value from having the AG able to speak to members about them. The second reason is this: if you have a system where any politician can object to the AG speaking, the likelihood is that, if what the AG is saying is going to be contrary to that member's point of view, then the member will probably object and say that the AG is stepping outside the bounds of what he is allowed to say. That would politicise the role of the Attorney General in a way which would be entirely undesirable and be capable of inhibiting the AG from saying things which he ought to say. Currently, even with a theoretically unfettered right to speak, I am very careful and cautious in regulating what I say, and sometimes this may not necessarily deliver the best value to the Assembly.

I then asked William Bailhache what he considered were the important challenges which the Island now faced. At the core of them he singled out growing global internationalisation.

> More and more international conventions and treaties are having an impact on what jurisdictions have to do domestically. In the old days treaties were made when you wanted to make trade or war or peace; today they are likely to be about regulating your

environment or your internal financial services or indeed a whole range of matters essentially domestic. And when these treaties are being made by the UK on our behalf, then there is the potential for difficulties, with implications which may not have been thoroughly considered. The United Kingdom itself comes under pressure from other countries especially as its relationship changes within the EU – why don't you make your territories and dependencies do what you say should be done? So the UK encounters these difficulties. And few outside understand the relationship between the UK and Jersey. On the one level there would be a big commitment if Jersey plays on the big stage; and yet there is another worry if we neglect the big stage and fail to address the problems of internationalisation as they affect our Island government.

And this is a related issue: the Kilbrandon commission some years ago stated that ultimately the UK parliament has the legal right to legislate on behalf of the Islands if it chooses to do so. We would say that that is not correct. We have no representatives at Westminster; the UK has never conquered us – it's the other way round. The matter has not been tested, and nobody wants to test it. Constitutional law has moved on since Kilbrandon's time, including the incorporation into domestic law of the European convention of human rights, both in the UK and in Jersey. So getting the balance right about how we relate to and deal with the outside world is a big challenge.

It had been a fascinating insight into some of the Island's current problems and the involvement of the Attorney General in them. I brought William Bailhache back finally to consider the Island where most of his life has been spent.

You ask what Jersey means to me. When I come back to the Island, when I fly over it and look down, I think, 'That's mine. That's where I belong.' And what's special about this part of the coast? I no longer have a boat – it went to France on its own last year and was ruined. I have been too busy to get round to replacing it. But one day, assuming I get to retirement, I shall buy another boat and take up where I left off.

~

I was now at the south-east corner of Jersey and turning sharp west, but there was time to take in the charm of La Rocque, a typical fishermen's harbour with its sea walls reputedly the oldest in the Island, and to walk out along its 19th century granite pier. A slate plaque at the shore end of the breakwater indicates a particularly significant historical event:

> **BATTLE OF JERSEY**
> **JANUARY 6TH 1781**
> **THE FRENCH TROOPS UNDER THE COMMAND OF**
> **BARON DE RULLECOURT**
> **CAME ASHORE HERE**

This was the Island's last French invasion: a force of 1200 men in 30 small boats creeping along the gullies in the dark of a winter night, capturing a nearby guardhouse and with 700 of them subsequently marching on to St Helier.

~

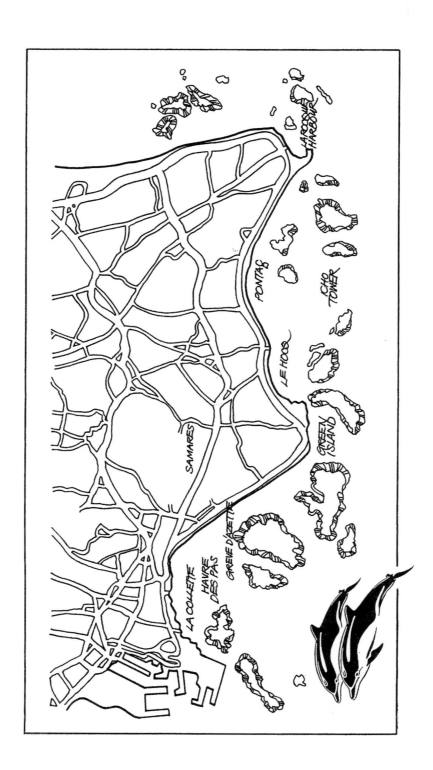

12

La Rocque to St Helier

The four or so miles from La Rocque Harbour in to Town cannot be said to be the most thrilling of the 48 round Jersey's coast, and the choice for the walker has to be shore or road, since there is no coast path and housing of many periods – charming 19th century cottages such as Summerleigh and Louvain, owned by the National Trust for Jersey, distinguished Victorian properties like Chateau La Rocque overlooking the harbour, much development from the 1930s up to the present day – have removed what would have been for all not living on the sea side the fascination of and contact with this unique rocky shore.

After half a mile or so I noticed a house on the left, The Cottage. It too has a slate plaque which states:

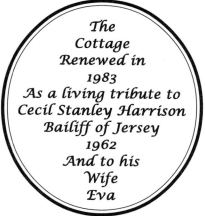

*The
Cottage
Renewed in
1983
As a living tribute to
Cecil Stanley Harrison
Bailiff of Jersey
1962
And to his
Wife
Eva*

I rang the bell and called in to see their daughter, Jurat Sally Le Brocq, who with her husband Philip now lives here. She gave me a cup of coffee and told me that The Cottage had been her parents' home from their marriage in 1927. She had spent the first two years of her life here, having been born in

1938. Her father, by this time Solicitor General, had acquired a larger house at Pontac further along the road, and there they moved while letting this property. Sally spoke to me of early memories.

> I was seven when the Occupation ended. I have memories of it but didn't realise how appalling it all was, having known nothing else. I do remember my mother missing a decent cup of tea, and shoes and clothes were passed on to me from others. It was cold at times, with nothing to burn.
>
> In my youth the sea on this coast meant a lot to me, and my father and I loved an early morning swim before breakfast and school. And if the tide was out, then it would be Anne Port instead.

Sally then told me about her time at Jersey College for Girls (in due course Head Girl), Exeter University (a degree in English, French and Latin), her father's progression to Attorney General and Deputy Bailiff and then his period as Bailiff before his sad death a few months later from cancer at the age of 59. She married Philip in 1963 and entered fully into and shared his life as a housemaster at Eastbourne College. There they brought up their four children and had to bear the heartbreak of the sudden and tragic death of their 16-year old elder son John in November 1980. Philip took early retirement in 1988 and they returned to Jersey and to The Cottage.

> Coming back wasn't terribly easy. It was another parting, a great wrench, since Eastbourne held all sorts of memories of John and was where we had brought up our family. But we both became involved, Philip running his leadership courses at schools in England and I with Victim Support, having been persuaded by Betty Brooke to set up a branch here in Jersey.
>
> Then, having been approached on three occasions, I stood for election as a Jurat and was sworn in in February 1997. There are many satisfactions and rewards in holding such an historic office but we get involved in heart-rending and emotionally involving cases - particularly young people caught up in the drug scene, with lives ruined and often threatened.
>
> The Jurats have the task in the Royal Court of determining guilt or innocence and the appropriate sentence. It is satisfying, yes; but it is demanding and exhausting at times, dealing with very human situations and with those so often from deprived

and sad backgrounds.

In July 2004 I was appointed one of the two Lieutenant Bailiffs, standing in for the Bailiff at times on ceremonial occasions and presiding on Friday afternoons over what is called the Samedi Court when contracts are passed.

I had learned much and rounded off our conversation by asking Sally what this particular spot, with the ever-changing sea at the bottom of her garden, meant to her.

> The sound of the sea is so important, and you pull back the curtains in the morning and there it is. Our garden is fairly modest but we have achieved much despite the south-westerly gales coming in and burning everything with salt. We have built out a little deck where we can go down on a summer evening, perhaps a glass of wine in hand, and see the sunset. And I swim regularly: on Liberation Day, even if it is a quick submerging, I have my first dip, and I go on into October. It is the variety of it all along this coastline that fascinates: the lunar landscape and then the incoming tide covering it twice every twenty-four hours.

~

It was not the best of weather and, on leaving The Cottage, I chose the road rather than the beach and plodded along the pavement past all sorts of properties, including a shop and a filling station, to Pontac. This is the first point after the harbour at La Rocque where the housing on the south side gives way to grass (not much more than a patch of it), allowing a panorama of the coastal scene with Icho Tower, built later than Seymour, occupying centre-stage. Just past the slipway here, a house lies on the north side, set back from the road. This is where Charles and Louise Blampied live, and I called in for a chat. Charles, son of Jurat Peter Blampied, though born in London has been here most of his life. As a boy he lived along the coast between Le Hocq and Green Island and he spent much of his childhood summers on the beach at Havre des Fontaines where, as the name implies, the fresh water bubbles up through the sand. The family had a little clinker boat and swimming and fishing and picnicking at Icho Tower, often with the Bailhache family who lived close by, were summer pastimes. He went to school at Charterhouse and then read Accountancy at the University of Kent at Canterbury. He qualified as a chartered accountant with Cooper Brothers and came back to work for them in Jersey – for the next 25 years until retirement.

Louise, with English parents, was born in South Africa and spent her life there, except for a few years in New Zealand, before coming to Jersey in 1986. Home was in St Brelade and she is honest in saying that in those days she thought the part of the Island where she now lives was 'absolutely ghastly', imagining headless riders emerging through the mists and across the rocks. She claims that it was 'quite something to move this side of the Tunnel'. At this point in our conversation Charles chipped in to say that he had had an aunt who thought that the only place to live was La Rocque and that it was very non-U to reside the other side, west of the Tunnel. Louise, who married Charles six years ago then added, 'I only got to know this side of the Island since I have known Charles, and I have to admit that I also thought St Ouen's Bay pretty hideous when I first came to Jersey. So unlike South African beaches. In the Island one becomes quite territorial.' I now quizzed Charles on the appeal of this south-east coast.

> The pull of it is partly roots – hankering for the place of one's childhood. I love the sea. Here you feel the wind and the storms and the calm days. And there is the fascination with the movement of the tides through the days – each different, depending on the spring tides or the neaps. We keep a little boat along from here in front of Dad's house and we use it mainly to go to the Ecrehos, navigating through all this rocky area round Le Hocq and La Rocque which from boyhood I know fairly intimately. At high tide virtually no rocks are visible. At low tide it is as if one is in a series of lagoons, little gullies and canals, with sandy bits tantalisingly exposed for an hour or so around low water.
>
> And another attraction for us is the huge variety of winter birds which most people never notice: these winter migrants – the Brent geese, but also grebes, divers, curlews, redshanks and so on. Sometimes at night we hear them roosting on the rocks and making a terrible din.

And had Louise come to terms with this coastline?

> Yes, I think so. It's the variety and one cannot get bored. The sea is never the same nor is the beach. Charles is actually a frustrated scavenger: he loves picking up bits of flotsam and jetsam, despite being irritated by all the junk which the fishermen throw over

the sides of their boats. My only regret is that we don't swim enough in the sea, but we are a bit dubious about the two outfalls by the slipway here and what may come out of them. And I share Charles's interest in the bird life. We are not quite twitchers but love the variety here and belong to the various bird societies.

Another attraction for me is the fact that my two sons who live in England adore fishing. They are mad about it and, given half a chance, they would come home every weekend to fish in the gullies here. Charles spent his childhood fishing but somehow didn't pick up all the skills and we therefore don't have a freezer full of fish.

Before I left Charles and Louise I asked them, Louise in Jersey for a couple of decades and Charles with deep Island family ties and most of his life here, for their thoughts and reflections on the Island now and in the future. Louise said this.

If you start getting too vociferous about it you get cranky and obsessive, and it doesn't make any difference. On the other hand I don't like burying my head in the sand. All I can do is vote when there is an election for someone standing who shares my values. But I do not like the waterfront development nor the proliferation of flats. Jersey seems to have become apartment-land – glorified ghettos in the making. We have some wonderful people in the States but they are a small minority. But despite all this, Jersey is a marvellous place to live and we are lucky to do so. But it's not cheap and I worry about the building that goes on and the number of office blocks that go up.

Charles added his comments.

I believe that the future of Jersey lies in the calibre of our politicians, and in my view that has deteriorated since they received a substantial salary. I much preferred the old honorary system of service. And then there is the personalisation of politics: I deplore the personal attacks of politicians – destructive and pointless. You have some politicians doing their best in a difficult world environment, trying to sustain the finance industry, and others bent on denigrating them. Long-term this could be very harmful for the Island. We once had a good system that worked well and I really deplore Clothier and everything else that's coming.

~

I left the Blampieds, having been told an interesting fact by Charles in response to my moan concerning the over-development of this St Clement coastline – that it was all because of the railway which ran along the shore from Town to Gorey; with the railway had come the house-building. It was therefore with some relief that I quickly reached Le Hocq, where the St Clement parish hall is located, and was able to appreciate again another area free of buildings to the south where I could once more take in the impressive rockscape of this special shore.

Fairly soon after Le Hocq I found myself passing Brig-Y-Don. I had often heard of this children's home and wanted to learn more. I rang the bell and was welcomed by Margaret Holley. She is Jersey-born, worked in London for quite a while after training as a nursery nurse and was appointed Head of Home in 1973. She also told me that she now had only six weeks to go before retirement. I asked her how Brig-Y-Don had started and I learned that the house had been owned by Trevor Matthews and given by him as a children's convalescent home in 1926 when tuberculosis was prevalent. As TB receded, so the home's purpose was modified. Margaret told me more.

> When I first came here we had lots of small babies who were failing to thrive, with some being rehabilitated back home and others being fostered. The main reason now for children coming into care is because of difficulties at home, with parents unable to look after them – social reasons. Our aim is always to get them back home; if not, then replacement families are sought. We try not to keep them for ever and a day, because this is not home, even though it is as pleasant as possible. But children thrive best in families; there's no doubt about that. At present we have nine children on the resident side and five in outreach – children who have been with us and who still need our support for a while. Our youngest child is two and our eldest sixteen. She's a lovely girl and has been with us since she was 18 months old. She's at school at Le Rocquier and we hope that, when she leaves, a family will befriend her and keep a supportive eye on her. We have a grant from Health and Social Services but we are not a States institution. We're charity-based, with a board of trustees, and we still need appeals and fund-raising to meet our costs.

As I was listening to Margaret I noticed the big garden at the back and the sight of the sea beyond. I asked what part they played in the work of Brig-Y-Don.

> It's a traumatic event when any child comes into care – a lot of heartache – and we find that the garden and the beach are great pluses. The children can relax that bit more and find some personal space. We had one little boy who was very troubled, and there is nothing he likes better - and he's been with us two and a half years – than to go into the rock pools with his fishing net. That has given him his time alone. He wasn't in tune with himself and he would argue and fight with the other children, and the beach has been his saving, as he is absorbed for a couple of hours with his net. He's much more relaxed now. And we also go as a group: picnics in the summer, finding shells, swimming and paddling.

Finally Margaret told me something of the pre-school group at Brig-Y-Don which operates from Mondays to Fridays in term-time but closes at 4 when the resident children are back from school and need the space. I also asked her about her retirement plans. She claims not to have given the matter much thought but wonders about the possibility of working with young adults with learning difficulties. There is, however, no doubt that she will be a hard act to follow at this well-known children's home after more than three decades of admirable dedication and work, recognised with her being awarded an MBE in the 2005 New Year's honours list, among these less fortunate youngsters in the Island community.

~

Leaving Brig-Y-Don I soon reached Green Island (or La Motte), this aptly named grass-covered rock which is 200 feet long and surrounded by water at high tide. Placed recently by its car park is a plaque that tells a sad story:

> **Here on 3rd May 1942, Peter Hassall, Denis Audrain and Maurice Goold, aged 15, 16 and 17 attempted to escape the Occupation carrying plans of Island fortifications to aid the allies. The boat was swamped. Denis drowned and is buried in St Saviour's cemetery. Maurice and Peter were captured and deported to camps in Germany. Maurice died in 1943 and his remains were re-interred in the Howard Davis Park in 1997. Peter died in 1998. His ashes are scattered nearby. United again.**

A happier feature of this spot is the Green Island Restaurant. It was 11 a.m. and, in this last week before its winter closure, the waiters and chefs were gearing up for the lunchtime business. Alan Winch, the restaurant's owner and driving force, welcomed me with a cup of excellent coffee, sat me down at one of the so far unlaid tables and told me something about himself. Born in Grantham, he has been in the Island for nearly 30 years. He was much involved in the development of Chateau La Chaire at Rozel as a country-house hotel, remains a director of the company that owns it and acquired Green Island Restaurant in 1996.

I inherited it as a glorified café which was under-utilised in my view. I saw all the positives about the situation: a lovely beach supported by local people; a big car park over which I have no involvement; all just the right size for me to take on and manage. At first I didn't know what I was going to do with it, but over my years in Jersey I obviously knew a lot of people that dined out, and a bit of a following started from that. It has evolved, customer-driven, to what it is today: a little single-block building, not perhaps looking from the outside what, hopefully, people experience from the inside.

I was on holiday in the Mediterranean - Cyprus, the Greek islands, nice experiences by the sea - and I wanted to transport some of those feelings back here, and I thought that this location would be the right place for that. I guess the cooking style is a little bit Mediterranean with a modern twist and an emphasis on local produce, particularly the fish and shellfish and locally grown vegetables.

I quizzed Alan about the restaurant trade and he told me how the breathalyser had affected establishments in low population areas of the Island. He also explained how the staff situation had eased in the previous few years with the arrival of Polish nationals. 'They have filled a massive vacuum in the leisure industry,' he said. He went on to tell me more.

> Things are changing quite a lot. There are the fixed price menus in the restaurants through October and part of November. In Jersey we have high rents, high overheads with accommodation and wages, and inflation as well. Discounting cannot carry on and work in all restaurants for five or six months in the year and is not the way forward with, as a possible result, fewer restaurants in four or five years' time. Giving value is the way forward for me, and I have no doubt that we will be among the survivors. When we are cooking on a cheaper menu, we do not compromise on standards – the same chicken breast that is used for the à la carte and the same ingredients right across the board. If you start reducing quality, then that is the downward slope.

And there is no doubting Alan Winch's optimism.

> Jersey is one of the most exciting places to have a restaurant if it is in the right location. We have residents with high disposable incomes; we have excellent local ingredients. And think of the Island with its safety and lack of serious political problems. Reflect on other countries and see how lucky we are. Go away on holiday and fly back; come down Beaumont Hill from the airport, realise that you are home and sense your good fortune. Jersey has a massive future; there's been too much down-talking in the last few years. Yes, there are adjustments to be made, but everything is in place for the Island to meet with success over the next decade or two.

~

Having left Green Island, I was soon at Grève d'Azette and on my way to Havre des Pas, with big apartment blocks, the La Collette power station chimney and Fort Regent ahead. On my right were the Le Marais high-rise flats, and I had this thought that Jersey always seems to ape English architectural trends, but a few years on. We have our Kingston by-pass in Victoria Avenue, our Festival of Britain in the Fort Regent skyline and our tall London residential blocks in these unsightly, intrusive Le Marais towers. I needed to speak to a man whose expert eye for buildings and his thoughts on what has happened to the Island's townscape are well-known.

André Ferrari was born in St Helier in 1954, gained a degree in Art at Loughborough and has for many years been active as a campaigner on conservation issues. He has two important books to his credit: *Jersey's Lost Heritage* and *Jersey's Disappearing Heritage*. In our chat he first had germane comments to make about the huge modern residential piles that I passed before arriving at Havre des Pas.

> Take the Victor Hugo building. It is almost as though it has spawned 'sons of Victor Hugo': bigger and bigger blocks that try vaguely to emulate some of the styles at Havre des Pas. They look quite attractive from a distance, with a sort of jagged skyline, but the nearer you get the cruder they become. What results is the crushing banality of an area devoted to residential apartments. The old vitality of this holiday district has gone with their arrival and the loss of so many hotels.

I asked André to describe Havre des Pas, its early charm and more recent developments.

Embedded in the fabric of the district are a few of the old fishermen's cottages – small, functional, one-storey buildings. And then there are the houses dating from the Regency and Victorian periods – that slight sense of the seaside resort, almost of Brighton: the villas with their pretty ironwork and attractive frilly detail. See the quality of this detail in buildings such as the Ommaroo Hotel, with that added touch of French influence.

And what went wrong? In the

Light at Grève d'Azette

1960s tourism was booming and many hotels, which had started as fine buildings, were extended very crudely – box alterations added to roofs, sides and fronts. This coarsened the appearance of the area. Important details were lost and something of the picturesque has sadly gone.

Then there is the land reclamation a bit further on. Go down to the La Collette basin area and note the ugly rubble walls, with lumps of rock piled on top of each other. Compare these structures of 30 years ago to the fine harbour sea walls of the 19th century.

I was unable to resist asking André to broaden the scope of his remarks and give me his opinion on recent developments elsewhere in St Helier.

It is all a terrible disaster. Take the waterfront: after they went beyond dumping rubble, they were thinking of a master-plan which included the idea of views and vistas and so on. That was torn up almost immediately and political wrangling and compromise took over. What we have got now is the cinema, the leisure centre and all that – a dreadful blot. It is awful and we should be thinking of another master-plan which would see the demolition and replacement of the cinema and a better system than the underpass which splits the area from the town.

As to the Esplanade and its environs, there is a huge amount of cramming going on there. Will these high-density developments going up now be the slums of tomorrow? And look at the height of these new buildings. They are on such a big, sterile, lifeless scale, and the views of the sea are being blocked off from the rest of St Helier. Walk down New St John's Road and you will see what I am saying. Take Pier Road: you will hardly see St Aubin's Bay when the rest of the waterfront is developed.

St Helier has had a mass of new developments which are very much a curate's egg, with 'modern' going up for the sake of being modern rather than because it's necessarily good architecture. Sadly the town's quaint charm has been lost for ever.

~

Before leaving Havre des Pas I wanted to call on Sonia Hillsdon who lives high above the beach at Bingham Court. Her book, *The Visitors' Guide to Jersey*, has been a rich source of information for me on my round-the-Island tour. I had also heard that she was an inveterate swimmer – in the sea, not in the pool. She first told me about her early life.

> I was born in Croydon but with Yorkshire cousins. My grandfather was a Scargill (but definitely not related to Arthur). He was a headmaster in London and I inherited his love of teaching. I gained a London degree in English and first taught at Chichester High School. After the sad death of my first husband I obtained a teaching post at St Helier Girls' School but after two terms decided that I would work for myself, and that's how I started writing. I was actually the music correspondent of the *JEP* for eight years and my first book, *Jersey Witches, Ghosts and Traditions*, came out in 1984.

Tidal pool, Havre des Pas

Sonia also told me that she had discovered that primary school children in Jersey, if given a project, say, on Elizabeth Castle, would have to get their information from an adult book. So she set about writing booklets about the Island's history, a whole series financed by herself and illustrated by Geraint Jennings and now widely used in our schools. I then asked Sonia about her special affection for Havre des Pas.

> The wonderful thing about my home here is its closeness to the sea. I love the idea that Havre des Pas was the harbour of peace – the story that Our Lady came and made the waters quiet so that the boats would come to a calm landfall. Look out to sea here, see the rocks on either side and imagine that sense of haven if you had been out on a rough sea.
>
> I swim every day, probably from March onwards and into October. I change into my costume here. I have a towelling robe, sling a towel over my shoulder and out I go. Nothing to worry

about; none of that horrible business of changing on the beach. And I can swim at all tides; and with the water far out at low water, then it such fun to walk out to it.

This intrepid, happy bather had one final instruction for me as I turned off my Dictaphone: 'Don't forget to put in the giggles.' I haven't.

~

I now climbed the hill over Mount Bingham with the power station and its chimney dominating the scene in front of me. I wanted to see inside and knew just the man to ask. Peter Routier, keen singer in choirs and one of my fellow church bell-ringers, is Company Secretary of Jersey Electricity and he kindly made all the necessary arrangements, with David Killip, Production Manager, being our very experienced guide. I was taken up to the control room, the very nerve centre of power generation and distribution for Jersey and the Channel Islands electricity grid. It was almost a scene from *Dr Strangelove* (for those old enough to remember the film) with its banks of computers, screens, dials and flashing lights. I enquired how many people were on power station duty at, say, three in the morning, and was interested to learn that the answer was just two.

It was then a matter of donning hard hats and fitting ear plugs before entering the impressive turbine hall with its diesel generators, boilers and steam turbines. I cannot claim to have understood everything that I was told, but I learned much: that La Collette power station was built in 1965; that it was situated here to be in close proximity to the harbour for fuel deliveries and a constant supply of clean seawater for the condensers and other heat exchangers; that since 1984 most of the Island's demand for electricity is now met by imports from France; and that La Collette now fulfils more of a strategic role, a full back-up if there were a loss of power from European sources.

The tour ended, I had a chance to chat with Peter. He was born in Oxford of Jersey parents, with his father then stationed at RAF Abingdon, and educated at Dauntsey's School in Wiltshire and the University of Surrey where he read Engineering. He returned to the Island and joined JEC in 1986, gained Chartered Secretary qualifications and became Company Secretary in 1996. I asked him to fill me in about the company and its work.

JEC is a public limited company with a London Stock Exchange listing. The States of Jersey have a controlling interest, owning a majority of the shares. Before La Collette was commissioned in 1966 all the Island's electricity was generated up at Queen's Road. This station is a back-up but we do have the capacity to generate all Jersey's demands and more if necessary. Incidentally a second French link was put in in 2000; the cables come ashore at Archirondel. And electricity for Guernsey is supplied from France via Queen's Road, with a cable going across to our neighbours from Grève de Lecq.

Why from France? It is the cheaper option. The French have both nuclear and hydro-electric sources, and they don't have quite the same hang-ups as the British about nuclear power. And there is another point: Jersey has Kyoto obligations, and we are largely meeting these with our power coming from clean French sources. If we were buying it from coal-fired suppliers, then the situation would be different.

Power station chimney, La Collette

Peter, from his position in one of the Island's most prominent companies, has his finger on the pulse of public matters and, before making my farewells, I asked him how he saw the state of Jersey today. He did not mince his words.

> Politically the Island is in a bit of a mess, and trying to run it effectively by consensus isn't working. In my opinion we need some sort of organised politics, and I believe that a political party system is the way forward. At the moment individuals standing for office produce these manifestos, but with the hope of their delivering them non-existent. Why don't they get on with the Clothier reforms and give us clear leadership? Most forms of government would be better than what we have at present. There seems to be universal disdain for a political system that has lost credibility.
>
> Fortunately the Island is bigger than the politicians that run it. So I believe that we will progress despite their best endeavours. But we are heavily reliant on the finance industry and we cannot afford to lose it. We must make sure of this; it is critical to Jersey's future.

~

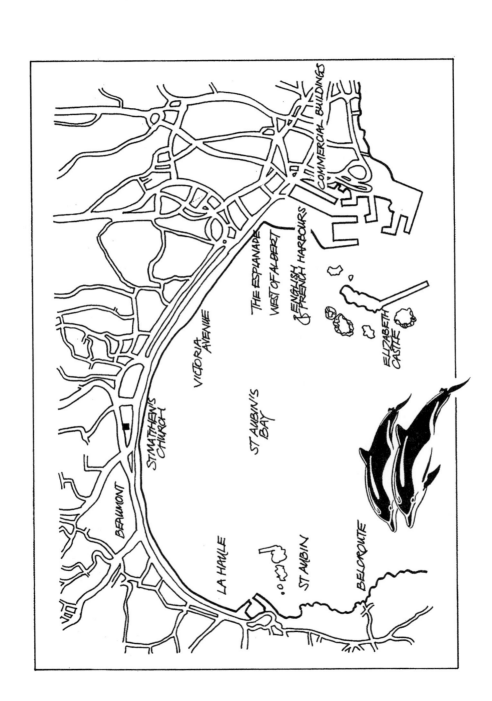

COMMERCIAL BUILDINGS

THE ESPLANADE
WEST OF ALBERT

ENGLISH
& FRENCH HARBOURS

ELIZABETH CASTLE

VICTORIA AVENUE

ST. MATHEW'S CHURCH

ST AUBIN'S BAY

BEAUMONT

LA HAULE

ST AUBIN

BELCROUTE

13

St Helier to St Aubin

As I left the power station I was only a few steps away from the home of the States' Planning and Building Services and, keenly remembering a lecture delivered by him a few years ago during Jersey's Architecture Week, I called in to have a chat with Stuart Fell, Assistant Director for Conservation. Stuart is a Cumbrian who went on to qualify as an architect in Leeds. He held various posts, including that of Conservation Officer in Chester, before coming to take up his Jersey post in 1995 where he heads the department's design and conservation section or, in other words, the historic buildings team. He took me on a fascinating verbal tour of the half-mile or so that lay ahead for me.

In Commercial Buildings we have one of the most interesting historic groups of buildings in the town, with its frontage on the English and French Harbours, dating from the early 19th century, evidently built as merchants' houses with warehousing behind. These fine, very prominent buildings have been quite seriously damaged in the last few decades through a combination of demolition, alterations and other changes, and a great deal of tender, loving care will be needed to restore their quality. We've made a start by giving grant assistance towards restoration work on one of the residential properties. Now that the Waterfront Enterprise Board is also keen to improve this area there are better prospects for positive change. The challenge here is to find the

English Harbour

optimum balance between heritage conservation, tourism and commercial interests, given that these properties accommodate thriving retail and service activities but also form the backcloth to the town's historic waterfront.

Then there's the Weighbridge. With the imminent move of the bus station to the Island Site, the potential of the Weighbridge as a public open space can at last be realised. This area is pivotal in linking the town – the parish church area and environs – to the waterfront. The key problem of course is the dual carriageway and how to tame it. This will be a major factor if the waterfront is to be successfully integrated with the old town; getting over the busy road in comfort is a critical objective, and one that many other waterside cities are having to grapple with.

I then asked Stuart about the old abattoir, with its preservation having been a cause close to his heart.

This complex includes one of the most important building groups in Jersey. There are few equals in Europe, as historic public abattoirs are not a very common building type. Here we have one of the best surviving abattoirs in the British Isles, which tells us a great deal about Jersey's commerce in the 19th century. It was therefore important that we did our best to save its character. In this we have mostly succeeded, the only loss being the slaughterhouse hall which will be diagonally cut in half to make way for the new transport interchange. Again, it's a matter of balance – in this case between affordability, getting the right uses to enhance this part of the town and bringing off good conservation work.

Stuart also made some interesting comments about the Esplanade, agreeing that in some areas it had lost much of its former attractiveness as a result of the office developments of recent years, but pointing out that such buildings had for their purpose to be modern and of a certain scale and size. I also wanted him to comment on a special interest of mine, the reclaimed land which had been the subject of my book published in 2001, *Hotel West of Albert: Jersey's Waterfront Saga*.

It is no secret that there were lively exchanges of view and opinion between the States planning committee and WEB who are charged with developing the west of Albert area. The committee's view was that the development should be design-led and guided by an agreed master-plan; WEB believed that their job was to get things built at least cost to the public purse, with the appearance of the area being best left to individual developers. Fortunately the two agencies are now in total agreement that the appearance, quality and feel of the area are fundamental objectives. The situation has massively improved, and future development should be more respectful of issues of design and character. In matters as subjective as design, however, it is impossible to please everyone.

You mention the cinema complex. Well, I have heard it described as one of the least satisfactory modern buildings in the Island, and I am not going to argue with that. It fulfils its function for the present; time moves on and all buildings get replaced sooner or later. And it is important to recognise that parts of the west of Albert development are potentially very exciting, and in the next ten, twenty years it will all come together. You've got to be a little patient and generous – towns take time to evolve.

Cineworld, Waterfront

Finally I asked Stuart what in his sphere he saw as the big issues ahead.

The biggest challenge is in accommodating the insistent pressure for new development. This has always been an issue in Jersey because of its modest size and shortage of building land. We need to provide new housing and commercial accommodation; we have to attract and retain business; and this puts pressure on infrastructure and can lead to development of questionable quality. We have to balance all these things and at the same time enhance and not damage the unique character of the Island. Much depends on the people of Jersey; if they vociferously demand high quality, then it is more likely that politicians will heed them. If people clamour and campaign and express views about these issues, then politicians will respond. If it is clear that people don't care, then standards will inevitably fall.

~

I was now on the home stretch, three or so miles from where I had started my journey at St Aubin, but unable without some pause to pass the developments on the waterfront 'west of Albert'. The reclamation of this area had started in 1979, and plans for a hotel on the site had encountered much public opposition. There was as yet no hotel, but the flats, the cinema, the pool, the night club and the fast-food outlets loomed large. It was opportune for me to seek out the managing director of the Waterfront Enterprise Board and enquire about its achievements so far and its vision for the future. David Margason, WEB's managing director, met me in his very modern set of offices on the Esplanade, and we chatted in his boardroom with its picture windows overlooking the waterfront leisure complex, the design of which is, to put it bluntly, not to everyone's taste.

David graduated as a civil engineer, working in Bristol and later in Gibraltar (he has a great passion for the sea and, with three others, sailed the Atlantic from there). He moved into construction, becoming a senior development manager for the Rank Organisation, active in developing casinos, holiday villages and the like. Later as a director of an Australian property company he was involved, among much else, in the development of the Blue Water shopping complex in Essex and at Darling Harbour in Sydney. The challenge to become involved in what he describes as 'one of the biggest waterfront developments in northern Europe' arose in 2003, and this is what brought him and his family to Jersey and to WEB in April of that year. I first wanted him to tell me what WEB actually is.

We are a limited company wholly owned by the States. All the shares are ultimately owned by the public. WEB is here to develop on behalf of the public the land assets that have been created by reclamation. It reports to the States Policy and Resources committee. We operate as a limited company in the way that we deal with finance, borrowing, taking risks and, increasingly, reducing our reliance on public funding to the point where it will soon be zero. WEB has administrative responsibility for west of Albert (and this includes Liberation Square and the bus station area) and an overseeing involvement in the development of a larger area encompassing the Harbour and La Collette.

I now quizzed David on his visionary plans for the future.

We need to create the premier short-break visitor destination in the Channel Islands. Think of St Malo, St Helier and St Peter Port as a three-legged triangle, with St Helier (mixed metaphors) as the cornerstone, the anchor. Imagine a family of five sitting in Swindon on a rainy January day. What is going through their minds for a holiday in choosing destinations A or B? What is Jersey's missing ingredient? Here is our unique opportunity to create a major addition to what we can offer. And our second aim is to provide the Channel Islands with its premier business centre, and we have a prime opportunity to do this.

We are starting to see the plan as a series of new public spaces or districts each of which has a particular purpose: the car-park site as the business centre; the marina frontage as the evening dining and leisure destination and with residential development as well; and the western part of the area as a family leisure village, set in a fabulous garden environment. We are getting together designers, funders and developers in partnership for each of these districts. Much, I hope, will be completed by 2009 with the office development perhaps by 2011.

Would there be a 'wow' factor in all this, I asked David.

Some people ask me where the iconic building is? Where is the Eiffel Tower or the Tenerife concert hall? We cannot expect the funding for such projects, but we do want to create a great visitor experience which collectively enhances what Jersey already has to offer. This will be a major public leisure destination which will be exciting and to which the public, I think, will respond positively. We would like to do something dramatic in terms of the architecture – something iconic, getting away from ground-scraping, monolithic construction, raising heights with a couple of architecturally bold moves. We would perhaps be failing if we did not attempt this.

And is David Margason relishing the challenge?

This will not be a single person's story. WEB is a facilitation organisation and our job is to mobilise the private sector and deliver visionary projects around our basic brief. It is really important that this half-completed scheme, which at the moment is viewed at best neutrally by people, now moves forward at a step-change pace. We are geared up and pushing for that to happen.

~

HSBC, The Esplanade

The Esplanade is the home to many of Jersey's finance houses, and a few doors along from David Margason's office is that part of the Barclay's Bank organisation where Justin Read, like me a member of Jersey's church bell-ringing fraternity, works. It seemed appropriate for me to have a chat with someone who has worked in Jersey's main industry – finance – for over a decade.

Justin is Dorset born and bred, from Blandford Forum. He joined Barclay's Bank at the age of 17 straight from school and worked at its branches in Poole and Blandford before having the opportunity of taking up a banking post in Jersey, moving here in 1993 on his 21st birthday, still 'a bit hung over' from the previous night's celebrations. In due course he was promoted into Barclay's premier banking division and is now a senior relationships manager. I asked him to tell me exactly what his job was.

> I have 300 clients, all of them from overseas. I am basically their bank manager. If they want to set up an investment portfolio, then I provide them with the advice or access to it. If they want to borrow money or wish to enquire about complicated tax structures, then they come to me. My job is to arrange facilities for the benefit of the client and at the same time to be challenged to increase our business.
>
> You ask about Jersey and the future of its finance industry. It is true that the computers could be turned off and easily transferred elsewhere, but you have to remember that Jersey and Barclay's have a very good brand, and the Jersey brand won't go. We are a top-tier finance centre, well regulated, staffed by sophisticated and highly qualified people, and operating within a stable governmental system. We are also in the right time zone: people in Africa, for instance, could not as easily do business with the Cayman Islands. We are in the middle of the world and this aids us in communicating readily with North America and the Far East.
>
> So our reputation is a strong one, and our future is assured at least in the short term. As to the longer term, I am not quite so optimistic. There are tax pressures: the European Union tax directive starts soon, and an EU resident will have 15% tax deducted from his interest and sent back to his country of residence. Then there is the OECD searching for tax harmonisation. We have a safe five years, but after that my crystal ball is a little hazy.

Justin is married to Louise, a chartered accountant, and they have a young daughter. Was Jersey to be the place where the family would happily stay?

> There is a financial advantage in our living here. Both of us are fortunate in having good rewarding jobs that, for our age, are better than we would expect in the UK. A move to the mainland would be a financial sacrifice. And the educational facilities for

our daughter when she starts school are of a high standard. I do moan about the local politicians, even writing to them occasionally, and some of them do not inspire confidence. I sometimes think that a few of our very good business people would manage the Island's economy better. Also higher calibre politicians would probably result in a more efficient civil service.

Yes, Jersey can be a bit claustrophobic and it is always good to get off the Island regularly. But Jersey has been good to me and I do feel a sense of loyalty to it. I am able to walk the half-hour to work in the mornings, dismiss the thought of London and commuting to a London office and think myself and my family fortunate indeed.

~

Victoria Avenue

Before moving west along Victoria Avenue I had one more person to meet, Advocate Richard Falle, whose plans in the 1980s for development at Havre des Pas had been thwarted and whose claims to the foreshore led to the controversial £10m settlement in 2003 between the States and Les Pas Developments Ltd. We chatted in the smart conference room at his offices, Bois and Bois, in Bond Street.

Richard comes from a Grouville farming family. He went to Victoria College and then on to Exeter College, Oxford, where he read English. His long-held ambition, however, was to become a lawyer and he was sworn in as an advocate of the Royal Court in 1968. Near the end of a long career Richard is today perhaps best known in legal circles for his knowledge of Jersey customary law. Over the years he has been associated with a number of conservationist causes, including the long drawn out fight against the flooding of the Island's valleys. He is a former President of the Société Jersiaise and was a founder member of the Jersey Heritage Trust. I wanted to find out more from Richard about the proposals of 1986 for a waterside development centred on a large marina at Havre des Pas and about the more recent matter of Les Pas and its settlement with the States.

The Havre des Pas scheme, inspired in part by my visiting Port Grimaud in the south of France, would have revitalised St Helier, drawn development and traffic away from the countryside and hugely benefited tourism. It was also inspired and underpinned by a long-held belief that the title to the foreshore (land covered and uncovered by the tides) was not, as commonly supposed, in the Crown but rather in the private ownership of the seigneur of a seaside fief. Over a long period I assembled a vast array of authority in support of this view.

Opposition to the scheme came from the Jersey Electricity Company which planned to build a coal-fired power station at La Collette. Our plans were clearly incompatible with those of the JEC and we demanded an environmental impact study and an examination of other energy options. The results of these studies which Les Pas vigorously supported eventually led the JEC to abandon a project potentially disastrous to the Island. To underpin our scheme it was necessary to secure a proprietary claim to the Havre des Pas foreshore, and Mrs Carole Hart, the Dame du fief de la Fosse, joined our association. Later, when Les Pas Holdings was incorporated, it acquired the rights in that fief.

In the autumn of 1986 the Crown officers were advised by me of the foreshore claim. We never expected it to go to court, but the then Solicitor General, Terry Sowden, was not willing to let the issue slumber on the file and instructed leading English counsel to prepare an opinion. Les Pas for its part also obtained a wholly contrary opinion from leading English counsel. By May 1992 Les Pas' plans seemed on the verge of acceptance, and we had made it clear that, if the project was given support by the politicians, then the legal claim to the foreshore beyond Havre des Pas would fall away. Three days after a very positive meeting with politicians and officials, we learned that a reconvened Policy and Resources committee had changed its mind and determined to end our dialogue. The Solicitor General too now refused all further discussion. His advice to the States was that the Les Pas case was 'entirely without merit'. Given the very different advice it had received Les Pas had little alternative but to accept the challenge and bring its summons to court.

Years later in 2001 Howard Page QC was commissioned by the Bailiff to manage the case and bring it to trial. His first adjudication concerned a preliminary application by the Crown and the States seeking an order for Security for Costs. The application was rejected. Only then perhaps did it occur to States Members that the result might be in doubt and they had to contemplate the risk of losing the case altogether. It was against this background that a settlement was reached.

As many will know, the settlement became something of a *cause célèbre* in the media and throughout the Island, with a body of opinion considering that the matter should have gone to trial and not have been settled. I asked Richard to reflect on the whole saga.

It has been a huge disappointment that our vision at Havre des Pas could not be fulfilled. I also have mixed feelings about the waterfront development west of Albert; most is banal and lacking in soul. It has certainly not followed the philosophy on which our own plans were based. Yes, the intellectual excitement of the legal case was some kind of compensation – with so many issues relating to Jersey law and the exploration of hitherto untouched bits of Jersey history. There has been some satisfaction, indeed vindication, in the ratification by the States of the settlement. I no longer hear the phrase 'a case without merit' bandied about. Had the matter gone to trial, there would have been, in the words of the Oracle, 'a great victory'.

Looking back on it all, a matter that has occupied so much of my time over almost two decades, I cannot see how we could have proceeded otherwise. My regret is that we did not reach a settlement that would have allowed us to go ahead at Havre des Pas, with all the benefits that would have accrued to the Island. A great opportunity was missed.

~

I now stepped out along Victoria Avenue, that ugly and unseemly approach to Town from the west. (Who was it that decided to place such an unfortunate suburban-style dual-carriageway by the edge of Jersey's impressively large southern bay?) And yet it serves well as the setting for the Island's big summer carnival, the Battle of Flowers, and it was to its Association headquarters in St Lawrence that I now went in order to talk to Bob Pallot, the chairman, and Terry Avery, its executive officer.

Bob was once a grower and now works for one of Jersey's produce marketing companies in its technical division. He has been involved in the Battle of Flowers for close on 40 years, from an initial involvement with the St Martin youth club. Later he became chairman of the St Martin Battle of Flowers organisation, with the parish twice winning the *Prix d'Honneur*. He then joined the Association council, later becoming vice-chairman and, in 2004, chairman.

Unlike Bob Pallot, Terry Avery is not a Jerseyman but a Londoner and an environmental engineer. But he has been in the Island for 40 years and the Association's executive officer for the last 20. I first asked Terry about the Battle's history in recent times. What about those little difficulties that not so long ago were extensively reported by the local media?

> There are always some personality problems. I have served seven chairmen in all and they have all been different. My job is a great one for trying to understand people. And we have had political problems, primarily to do with money. The politicians seem slow to realise what the Battle means to Jersey and its people. They've taken the matter too lightly. The problem is cash, cash, cash, and, with the tourism industry decimated in the last few years, our income has been reduced.
>
> And how has the Battle changed over the last few years? It has got better; the floats are these days superb, no longer just a block of flowers. They are tableaux with everything moving on them, with dancers and music. The exhibitors must surely be producing the finest floats in the world.

Bob now took over and told me about his thoughts for the future.

> We are reverting to the two-pass parade, part of the Jersey tradition, having tried it going only one way. And the Association council would like a free parade, and it is finance that holds us

back. If the parade were free, then the whole Island could attend it, and every tourist would come too. Some politicians are interested in the idea, and a major sponsor would mean our going a long way to realising this dream. A free parade would get the locals back to the Battle, and there would be the prospect of creating a celebration week - Battle Week, Jersey's carnival.

As to moving the Battle to the weekend, I am in favour of retaining Thursday, with the popular moonlight parade on the Friday evening. The trouble with a weekend Battle is that people don't like change and they have their own weekend hobbies and family activities then.

Some want us once again to have a Mr Battle. It would be great, but the problem with this is the sheer cost. In the last years of our having a Mr Battle we were getting the lower end of the celebrity range, and people don't want that.

At this point Terry chipped in to tell me that the last major celebrity as Mr Battle had been Ian Botham but that he had cost a total of £14,000. I invited him and Bob to sum up and give me their big thoughts. Terry said this:

My big thought is that the government of the Island should understand the value of the Battle and should come on board and support us. Support all the voluntary effort that goes into it and give us the necessary resources. Or they should come along and say that this is the end of the Battle and cut the cord. We want the States to come on our side and promote us.

Bob echoed these sentiments:

People forget the huge community involvement in the Battle: 25 to 30 floats each year; up to 12 parish floats; another few 45 ft floats; 50 to 100 people occupied in flowering and constructing them; multiply that by 25 to 30 and you see the community input.

The Battle has been in existence for over 100 years. It is one of the top parades in Europe or the world. This is what a little island has achieved and, apart from two paid Association staff, it is all done for free, done for the love of the Battle and the love of Jersey. This is what the States should remember and why that extra financial backing would take the Battle of Flowers forward into the future.

~

As I approached Bel Royal I felt compelled to divert slightly and, for the first time in many years, visit St Matthew's, Jersey's famous 'glass' church, which lies a field's breadth back from the dual carriageway. It was first consecrated in 1840 as a chapel of ease for the inhabitants of Millbrook, unable or unwilling to travel up the hill to the parish church of St Lawrence. But it was in 1934 that Lady Trent, widow of Jesse Boot, the founder of Boots The Chemist, commissioned René Lalique to refurbish the interior of St Matthew's in memory of her husband. This he did in collaboration with local architect A.B.Grayson. The result is surely both stunning and virtually unique, with Lalique's moulded white glass used for much of the furniture which would normally be in wood and stone. It is little surprise that the church is a Mecca for the summer tourist coaches and a flood of visitors who come to see the fluted glass of the font, the windows, the screens, the frosted silver glass panels of the communion table and, behind it, the magnificent glass cross – the focal point of the interior – standing over four metres high. On this winter afternoon I had the church and its marvels to myself. I decided to seek out the Reverend Phil Warren who since November 2003 has been Rector of St Lawrence and also (it goes with the appointment) Vicar of St Matthew's and was welcomed into his office in a brand-new rectory behind the parish church and built next door to the older one, recently sold.

I wanted to know more about St Matthew's but first wished to learn something of the parish's new Rector. He is the son of an archdeacon and spent his formative years in south London, going to school at St John's, Leatherhead, gaining an honours degree in History and Religious Studies and teaching for ten years, first at Alleyn's School and then, as head of RS and Philosophy, at Latymer Upper in Hammersmith.

> In my last two years of teaching I really felt God calling me to the Anglican ministry, went to theological college in Nottingham, got ordained at Southwark Cathedral and was a curate for three years at St Mary's, Reigate. Then out of the blue I received a phone call from the Dean of Jersey wondering whether I would be interested in coming here. Now I have to make a confession: my wife's father is a Guernseyman, and the only time that I had ever been to Jersey before was when there was fog with the plane diverted. So my first response to the Dean was 'nice idea, but wrong island'. After 18 months here I know that it was I and not the island that was wrong.

Engaged with Phil's story and putting St Matthew's and its glass for the time being on one side, I asked the Rector about the challenges and responsibilities of his first year and a half in St Lawrence.

It has been very different from the role of a clergyman in England and a steep learning curve. But the Constable and I have a great working relationship and, with my theology of church being very much community-based, I welcome my involvement in the civic life of the parish and the opportunities that this brings.

Now concerning St Matthew's, I knew nothing about it before arriving in Jersey, having imagined a church with a great glass front, literally a glass church. I think I was taken aback when I first saw the incredible art deco glass inside and I have grown to love it. An acquired taste perhaps. What really struck me was when I did my first baptism, realising that the font must be quite unique. I believe that God does bless the time and energy that goes into a place, the skills that brought this about. There is something special that takes place within an act of worship here.

Phil then told me how he and his wife and their two daughters had settled into their new life in Jersey.

People have shown an enormous warmth to us. We feel very much part of the community, and I am passionate about St Lawrence being the best parish in the Island – part of my competitive nature. I love the parish and its people.

And Jersey is beautiful. Now, friends back in England think of the Island as being all millionaires as portrayed in *Bergerac*. But there are small houses, with both parents having to work to pay the mortgage, and as much suffering, pain, loneliness, depression here as elsewhere. Indeed I have experienced more extreme pastoral problems here than I ever did in England. There is a great need for God; people need to hear the Gospel and know God's love as much here as anywhere else.

Also it has been interesting for me to pick up Jersey's current political and economic dynamics; there will be changes, good or bad, and it will be challenging for me to be part of this. And spiritually these are exciting times, with the churches working more closely together than ever before, and this is a good sign.

As to St Lawrence and St Matthew's, the one a country church and the other with a more urban mind set, we had a joint service on Plough Sunday, the first such for many years. I was reminded of Psalm 133: 'Behold how good and joyful a thing it is, brethren, to dwell together in unity'. It is exciting for me to be part of that.

~

Returning to Bel Royal, I strode along the path, avoiding cyclists and that sad mode of transport for the lazy tourist, Le Petit Train, towards Beaumont. This is the home of my wine merchants, Dunell's, and I popped into their big showroom to catch up with someone who, in this business, knows what he is talking about: Ilario Utichi.

Ilario grew up in a village not far from Parma – where the ham comes from – in the Po Valley. After national service in the Italian air force he came to Jersey in 1968 and has been here ever since. He has had much experience in the hotel and wine industry: first a barman at L'Horizon, then manager of The Moorings Hotel at Gorey, involved in the formation of Victor Hugo Wines and, with others, a partner in Vin Direct.

> Vin Direct, with its shop at L'Etacq, was very successful. People were coming from Gorey to buy our wines. With my knowledge I knew all the best producers in France, Spain and Italy, and we picked some extremely nice wines and sold them at a reasonable price. The company grew very fast and I was able, because of its success, to buy myself a house outright. I took a week off for the move and on the first day a lorry, going at 50 mph, hit the back of my car – the driver had had an epileptic fit – and this did a lot of harm to my back and neck. For a year and a half I was out of account.

Vin Direct was later sold and Ilario took a job at the Jersey Zoo's Café Dodo. This was for him a return to familiar territory since he had done v.i.p. catering in the 1970s for Gerald Durrell – 'He was a good friend of mine' – providing the food for Princess Anne, James Stewart, Michael Bentine and others of his prominent guests.

I now asked Ilario how he kept up to date with his knowledge of wines. He told me that his managing director at Dunell's, Neil Pinel, insisted that they tasted regularly.

> We get sent three to four dozen bottles a week from different

producers. So we taste them, and not just those wines being sent to us but those not tasted for three or four months – just to make sure. A half a glass of wine; we get the knowledge that way. And there's my hotel background: I can say to a customer, 'You tell me what you wish to eat with the wine and I shall give you the best bottle I have got for the price you wish to spend.' I know all the good bottles in the store, and our stock, some of it good wine from small producers, improves all the time.

I ended our chat by asking Ilario Utichi what, after 37 years here, Jersey meant to him.

It means a lot; it is very special. I have worked hard all these years but have enjoyed every minute of it. This cosmopolitan island is the best in the world as far as being nice to imports like myself. People have always been friendly from day one. And when I go in to Town I always find myself saying hello to 25 or 30 people within the hour. The Island community is second to none in making everybody feel welcome.

~

Emerging from Dunell's, I was now on the final lap, with half a mile of the 48 remaining. As I approached La Haule and its slipway, I looked across the field to the right and, above it, the handsome property, Mon Plaisir. Joan Stevens, in her *Old Jersey Houses, Volume II*, gives it three paragraphs and describes it in these terms: 'This delightful little "romantic" house, an early version of the modern split-level construction, was built by Philippe Marett of La Haule in about 1820'. I wanted to find out more and made a call on Philippe's great-great-granddaughter, Suzie Marett-Crosby, whose home it now is. The daughter of Sir Robert Marett, she welcomed me at the front door which is on the first floor level at the back and took me downstairs to the high-ceilinged drawing room with its splendid view over St Aubin's Bay. She had much to tell me about the house and the family.

My great-great-grandfather built Mon Plaisir because he loved the location with its sweeping views over the bay and its two majestic chestnut trees, one of which sadly fell last winter. Although he did live in the house, it was then rented out until my father retired in the 1960s and restored it. The family home was La Haule Manor.

Yes, Joan Stevens was right to describe it as "romantic". Lots of people have lived here, been married from it and spent their honeymoons here. And you will have noticed it is built on the slope of the *côtil*, and that is why you came in at the bedroom level and came downstairs to this room. There is a charming little coach-house behind, with a ship's bell on top which was used to summon the farm-workers. I have a deep affection for the house and for the furniture and paintings that were saved from La Haule Manor.

Mon Plaisir, La Haule

Suzie went on to tell me more about the Maretts. Her grandfather, brought up at La Haule Manor and educated at Victoria College, was Rector of Exeter College, Oxford. Her father was born in Oxford but spent the long months of the university vacations in Jersey. He had a varied and interesting life that included working for a commercial company in Brazil, marrying Suzie's mother, a Mexican brought up in New York, being a correspondent for *The Times*, moving into the diplomatic service and holding increasingly senior positions until his last posting as British Ambassador in Peru. His daughter continued the story:

On his coming back to Jersey in retirement he became States Deputy for St Brelade. It may sound strange but he was probably happier as a Deputy here in the parish than in any of his distinguished diplomatic posts. I believe that he contributed greatly to the States with his integrity and sense of vision. He loved 'coming home' to his beloved island after so many years abroad.

I now asked Suzie Marett-Crosby to tell me a little about herself and her life since coming to Jersey and to the lodge at La Haule Manor in the early 1970s.

> Through friends I moved into publishing, joining a firm that published and distributed academic books throughout the world. I also built up my own list of Jersey titles under the name, La Haule Books.
>
> I then taught the Open University humanities course for eight years and have just given that up. For a number of years I was a Samaritan, eventually becoming director of the local branch. I am now involved in helping to run parenting courses and, with a former Samaritan director, I have recently started a prison visiting scheme at La Moye.

If that was not enough, Suzie took part two years ago in Jersey Overseas Aid, engaged in a project to build accommodation for doctors at a clinic in Ecuador, with her taken on, she quickly told me, not for her practical construction skills but for her expertise as a fluent Spanish linguist. And she spoke too of her son, Michael, an alumnus of Ampleforth, an Oxford DPhil and currently a priest here in Jersey at St Thomas's, and of her daughter and son-in-law, both working at present in Jersey and living at Mon Plaisir.

~

This was an absorbing final encounter before my journey's end. Five minutes later I was outside the St Brelade parish hall where it had all started fifteen months previously. I was the wiser and, hopefully, the better for having tramped the coast and for having met so many of those who, with its island beauty, make Jersey a unique and special place.

~

More titles from Seaflower Books are as follows:

CHANNEL FISH: A Book of Fish Cookery from the Channel Islands
by Marguerite Paul
Our bestselling fish cookery book.
ISBN 0 903341 10 8; 24 pages; £9.95

ISLAND KITCHEN: A Book of Seasonal Cookery from the Channel Islands
by Marguerite Paul
Follow-up to 'Channel Fish', featuring seasonal produce, local and not-so-local recipes.
ISBN 0 903341 18 3; 192 pages; £9.95

JERSEY ALPHABET
by John Le Dain
From Abreuvoir to Zoo, essential notes on all things Jersey.
ISBN 0 948578 84 X; 128 pages; £4.95

JERSEY CYCLES
by Arthur Lamy
Explore the island, parish by parish, on two wheels. 12 routes for Jersey's 12 parishes.
ISBN 0 903341 11 6; 128 pages; £5.95

JERSEY HORSES FROM THE PAST
by John Jean
Pictorial presentation of the vital role our four-legged friends once played.
ISBN 0 903341 01 9; 96 pages; £4.95

JERSEY IN LONDON
by Brian Ahier Read
Story of the Jersey Society in London, which played a vital role during the war years.
ISBN 0 948578 64 5; 192 pages; £6.95

THE JERSEY LILY: The Life and Times of Lillie Langtry
by Sonia Hillsdon
Our second bestselling title.
ISBN 0 948578 55 6; 128 pages; £5.95

JERSEY: NOT QUITE BRITISH: The Rural History of a Singular People
by David Le Feuvre
Absorbing account of Jersey's rural heritage.
ISBN 1 903341 27 2; 160 pages; £6.95

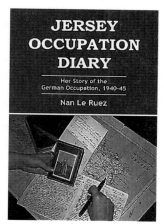

JERSEY OCCUPATION DIARY: Her Story of the German Occupation 1940-45
by Nan Le Ruez
First-hand account of one Jerseywoman's experience of the Occupation. Riveting reading.
ISBN 1 903341 19 1; 240 pages; £9.95

JERSEY OCCUPATION REMEMBERED
by Sonia Hillsdon
The Occupation experience, in the words of those who lived through it.
ISBN 1 903341 213; 160 pages; £5.95

JERSEY RAMBLES: Coast and Country
by John Le Dain
Latest edition of our perennial bestseller features new Jersey Coast-to-Coast walk.
ISBN 1 904431 26 4   128 pages; £5.95

JERSEY WEATHER AND TIDES
by Peter Manton
Jersey's weather sets records in the UK and its tides are some of the world's biggest. Learn more from this book.
ISBN 0 948578 75 0; 96 pages; £5.95

JERSEY WITCHES, GHOSTS & TRADITIONS
by Sonia Hillsdon
Ghoulies, ghosties and things that go bump in the night!
ISBN 1 903341 13 2; 160 pages; £6.50

JOHN SKINNER'S VISIT TO THE CHANNEL ISLANDS: August 1827
Edited by John Le Dain
Revealing journal of a short-break tourist to Guernsey and Jersey in 1827.
ISBN 1 903341 25 6; 20 pages; £2.50

LIFE ON SARK by Jennifer Cochrane
Tells what it is like to live throughout the year on
the Channel Island with the greatest mystique.
ISBN 0 948578 63 7   128 pages; £5.95

THE MOTOR CAR IN JERSEY
by David Scott Warren
This book tells the story of the motor car in the
island.
ISBN 0 948578 68 8   128 pages; £6.95

**PRISON WITHOUT BARS: Living in Jersey
under the German Occupation, 1940-45**
by Frank Keiller
Growing up as a teenager during the Occupation.
Exciting stuff!
ISBN 1 903341 00 0; 192 pages; £6.95

**GUERNSEY COUNTRY DIARY: Through the
Natural Year** with Nigel Jee
Informative, amusing and altogether delightful
account of the natural year in Guernsey.
ISBN 0 948578 90 4; 128 pages; £4.95

**NO CAUSE FOR PANIC: Channel Islands
Refugees, 1940-45**
by Brian Ahier Read
The story of the thousands who evacuated from
the islands prior to the arrival of the occupiers.
ISBN 0 948578 69 6; 160 pages; £6.95

**THE SEA WAS THEIR FORTUNE: A Maritime
History of the Channel Islands**
by Roy McLoughlin
The fascinating story of the Channel Islands'
maritime past.
ISBN 0 948578 86 6;160 pages; £5.95

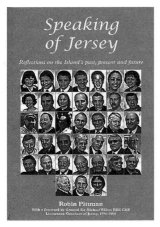

**SPEAKING OF JERSEY: Reflections on the
Island's Past, Present and Future**
by Robin Pittman
ISBN 1 903341 14 0; 224 pages; £7.95

WILD ISLAND: Jersey Nature Diary
by Peter Double
The natural year in Jersey, profusely and
beautifully illustrated.
ISBN 0 948578 77 7; 120 pages; £7.95

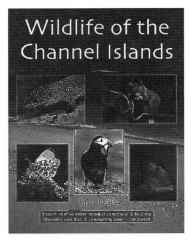

WILDLIFE OF THE CHANNEL ISLANDS
by Sue Daly
A beautiful and informative book featuring some
240 superb photographs in full-colour.
ISBN 1 903341 24 8; 221 pages; £14.95

**WISH YOU WERE HERE...
A Holiday History of Jersey seen through
picture postcards**
by John Le Dain
More than 250 Jersey postcards, many with holiday
messages, from the 1900s to the 1960s.
ISBN 1 903341 12 4; 192 pages; £9.95

*Seaflower Books are available through your local
bookshop or may be obtained direct from the
publisher, post-free, on receipt of net amount.*

SEAFLOWER BOOKS
16A New St John's Road
St Helier
Jersey   JE2 3LD

www.ex-librisbooks.co.uk